TOMMY LEADER

"BUTCH"

Sqdn/Ldr T.F. DALTON-MORGAN, D.F.C.   43 SQUADRON

ORDE
29/12/1941

Squadron Leader Tom Dalton-Morgan, DFC, by Cuthbert Orde

TOMMY LEADER

GROUP CAPTAIN TOM DALTON-MORGAN
DSO, OBE, DFC & BAR

WITH CLIVE WILLIAMS

FOREWORD BY

AIR COMMODORE P M BROTHERS
CBE, DSO, DFC & BAR

GRIFFON INTERNATIONAL

This edition published in 2007

PUBLISHED BY:
Griffon International plc
Griffon House
32 High Street, Wendover
Buckinghamshire HB22 6EA,
United Kingdom
Tel: ++44 (0)1296 620283
e-mail: sales@militarygallery.com

British Library Cataloguing in Publication Data.
A catalogue record for this book is available from the British Library.

ISBN 0 954997 01 8
ISBN 978-0-9549970-1-4

PRINTED AND BOUND IN UK

CONTENTS

FOREWORD

by Air Commodore P M Brothers
CBE, DSO, DFC & Bar

TOM MORGAN is a name to conjure with. Ace fighter pilot, Wing Leader, brilliant planner and staff officer, widely known and respected throughout the Royal Air Force before and during World War II and subsequently in the high-level civilian posts he occupied.

This autobiography is the fascinating story of a man whom I believed would rise to become the Chief of Air Staff. Although the period when we served together was, to my regret, relatively brief, such was the impact of his personality on me, that my belief became quickly apparent.

Perhaps some elucidation is due. Tom joined the RAF not long before me and whilst initially being involved in the Naval co-operation aspects, soon found his niche as a fighter pilot, by which time I was already a fighter pilot. The pilots of Fighter Command were a small close-knit club and whilst I had not met Tom, I knew some of his friends and had heard of him. He may even have heard of me. Hence, when we finally met and served together in November 1943 on the Headquarters Staff on No. 10 Group, a friendship was quickly established. He was the Group Captain 'Operations' working until the early hours planning the day's operations with the bomber forces. I was in charge of the training.

Early in December Tom had to go to hospital to sort out recurrent headaches and I took over his job. He returned after Christmas and I became the Exeter Wing Leader. In my new position I was in frequent contact with Tom over operational matters and, as I expected, could rely on his swift and unquestioning assistance. Our work together ceased when he was posted to 2nd Allies Tactical Air Force prior to the invasion of Europe.

I followed his career during the invasion with interest and noted that his movement from job to job invariably involved more responsibilities and importance, an upwards path as I expected, finishing in Germany. As I left the RAF for two years, I lost all contact with him and was surprised on my return to find that he had left the Service and emigrated to Australia. I heard rumours but had no confirmation until in the course of my duties, I made an enquiry about the Woomera Rocket Range and was told 'Tom Morgan runs that organisation. Only he can help you'. I knew you could not keep a good man down.

As always, life has its ups and downs. His story shows how personality, determination and leadership can make the 'ups' exceed the 'downs'.

INTRODUCTION

by Clive Williams

I FIRST met Tom at RAF Hendon in 1992 on the occasion of the launch of the second edition of *Aces High*. We immediately formed a rapport and friendship that resulted in the collaboration and subsequent publication of this book.

However, before the book could be completed, Tom passed away on the 18th September 2004 from liver cancer, which had been diagnosed three months earlier although, in retrospect, it was apparent that he had been suffering for some period of time. With the determination and courage, he had shown throughout his life, he kept it hidden with great fortitude until the end.

During his RAF career, for some time in 1944, he was unofficially attached to the US 8th Air Force but, because of the nature of the assignment, no apparent records were kept by the USAAF, and this part of his career is not covered in the book. However, research into this period of Tom's career is ongoing and, should further information be discovered, a second edition will be produced. As part of this research, as will be seen in the appendices and acknowledgements, there are many references to the US 8th Air Force.

Wherever possible I have tried to confirm engagements and claims from *Luftwaffe* records and, against most of the claims, I have noted the names of the Luftwaffe personnel involved.

Tom was an extremely modest and unassuming man and, during our time together spent compiling the manuscript, I often thought of saying, 'This is like extracting teeth.' His modesty is well illustrated in the many photographs that were taken of RAF and Battle of Britain functions that he attended after the war. If you look at the photographs, Tom will be found standing at the back or at the end of the line.

It was my privilege to have had Tom's friendship and to have assisted in this tribute to him.

Clive Williams

ACKNOWLEDGEMENTS

W E WOULD like to express our thanks to the many people who have given their time to assist with this work, particularly the following; Andrew Johannes Mathews, David Williams, Dave Cook, Colonel Bill Saavedra, USAF (Ret'd), Tom Lowery, Wing Commander Chris Goss, Simon Muggleton, Phillipa Hotchkiss, Claude Hellas, Tony Wood, R B Forbes-Morgan, Jonathan Sutherland, Tony Mansell, Stephen Bungay, Anne Clark, Air Commodore Graham Pitchfork, Bill Westlake, Andy Saunders and Alan Pollock.

We would also like to acknowledge the help of the following public bodies and associations; the Imperial War Museum, Public Record Office, RAF Museum Hendon, National Archives & Records Administration (USA), Association of the 4th Fighter Group, Air Force History Support Office, Bolling Air Force Base (USA), 43 Fighter Squadron 'The Fighting Cocks' Association, the Battle of Britain Association, RAF Ibsley Historical Group.

To Rick Taylor of the Aces High Gallery for the publication of this book, and Colin West for his technical help in the final preparation of the manuscript and its ultimate production. Also, to Dee Dalton Morgan for her continued enthusiasm for the project, her care of Tom's notes and records and her constant help and encouragement.

Finally, to Judy Williams for her assistance with typing and coping with the ever present mounds of paper about the house.

Sweeping squadrons
Filled the summer sky
White trails across the
Brilliant blue

We met them head on
Five miles high
They were many, we were few
Went the day well?

We died and never knew
But well or ill – freedom – we died for you
And left the vivid air
Signed with our honour

And now –
Do you remember us
They called The Few?
We need to know that
we are not alone
That here and now our
Sacrifice is known
And we are not forgotten

Anon.

CHAPTER ONE

Early Days;
First Flying Experience

A S A SMALL boy I used to like watching the different birds. I would try to identify them and their different characteristics. The way they approached to land and the way they took off. How they used their wings and the way they glided.

As I grew I became interested in the weather. The wind and changes in the temperature and weather patterns. Watching the birds and weather, I wanted to become part of this element. This ambition was fuelled by occasional flights in the aircraft of the flying circuses that moved around the country and conversations with the pilots.

At age seventeen, and at my last OTC camp at school there was talk of short service commissions in the Royal Air Force being offered to eligible personnel. Educationally, I appeared eligible. I had passed my Senior Cambridge Standard Exam and had been granted exemption from the Matriculation Examination.

At this time, I knew nothing of the Royal Air Force College at Cranwell. Otherwise I would have sought entry.

With advice, I wrote to the Air Ministry seeking information. In late 1934 I was granted an interview for a Short Service Commission. It seemed I passed the interview and subsequently the medical examination. Later I was notified that I had been accepted for a Short Service Commission but it would be some months before I would be called forward.

The Air Ministry sent me some useful books associated with aviation to study. I thought I would try to obtain some practical experience, so I visited the Cardiff Aeroplane

Club. The Club Secretary pointed me in the direction of the Chief Ground Engineer (CGE) in the aircraft hangar. He agreed to me working on a voluntary basis in the hangar under his strict supervision and that of his only aero-mechanic, Ivor, now called a Licensed Aircraft Maintenance Engineer.

At that time, the aerodrome, now called an airfield, was a small grass airfield. The Cardiff Aeroplane Club was the sole occupant. The club comprised a clubhouse and three staff, a flying instructor (ex RAF medium service officer), a Chief Ground Engineer and one aero-mechanic, one small hangar, two Gypsy Moths and one Tiger Moth.

The hangar also housed a World War I Avro 504K in flying condition. This aircraft was the personal property of a wealthy member of the club. It was personally maintained by the CGE. Ivor, the aero-mechanic and myself were the only allowed near it with the CGE.

The problem was how to get to the aerodrome on a reasonably regular basis. Public transport was not available all the way. The distance from where I lived near Penarth to the aerodrome was about eleven miles (approx 18 km). My bicycle was now too small. My younger brother, John, who was still away at school had a new Raleigh Roadster with three speed gears and a chain bar. To borrow his bike seemed the answer. So, except when the weather was too inclement, I set off each day with sandwiches. Hot coffee was always available in the clubhouse.

Penarth and its environs was located some 900-1,000ft above Cardiff coastal plain. So the ride to the aerodrome was downhill from home through pleasant countryside and across Cardiff city plain. The ride home involved the climb up the steep hill for some one or two miles. At the end of a days work, it was a very steep hill.

At the aerodrome I worked in the hangar under Ivor, the aero-mechanic. This included engine and airframe maintenance, control wire inspection and replacement and repair of aircraft fabric covering. It also included hand swinging the aircrews to start the engines for flight. In all that I did, Ivor was always a helpful teacher and cheerful and pleasant companion. Later, when I was in the RAF and home on leave he helped me overhaul the engine of my first car, a Crossley.

One morning before flying started the CGE told me to take the fire engine, an old Dennis, around the aerodrome perimeter for its daily test run. I explained that I had not yet driven a vehicle. My father had not yet allowed me to drive the family car. The CGE retorted, 'you will soon learn, my boy. Up in the driver's seat with you'. Whereupon he explained the controls and gears, told me to start up the engine and get going. I did.

Carefully I went through the old-fashioned gate gear change. I drove steadily around the perimeter of the grass aerodrome and returned to the parking bay for the fire engine near the hangar. I was met by the CGE and Ivor. The CGE said he had been watching me. In future, he continued, I would do the daily test run of the fire engine and be responsible for the maintenance of the fire engine and its equipment, under the guidance of Ivor.

After I had swung the propeller for him a few times, the flying instructor, formerly Flying Officer Pope, RAF, and I talked. He spoke of his life in the RAF. I listened with interest. He knew I was waiting to start service in the RAF and gave me much useful information. I spoke of my hobbies and how I was enjoying the few months at the aerodrome before being called forward to train as an officer pilot. From then on I was taken up on some of the daily test fights. I learnt the effect of controls, take-offs and the approach to landing. I was permitted to take the controls in the air. For take-offs and landings, which I did, Mr Pope remained hands-on, mainly because I was not a bone fide member. Before I left Cardiff aerodrome to commence my RAF initial training, Mr Pope said I was ready to go solo.

However, I soon became known to the owner of the Avro 504K. It had been converted to dual control. After pulling the prop to start the engine and removing the wheel chocks a few times, under the eagle eye of the CGE, he introduced me to the owner. The CGE explained my presence at the aerodrome. Later the owner of the Avro 504K asked me if I would like to fly in the aircraft. I said yes and climbed into the second cockpit before there was any change of mind.

There was a parachute already in the cockpit. The owner said not many chose to fly in the old aircraft. I flew with him several times in the 504K, including doing the take-offs and landings.

One day, after a short flight with me he got out of his cockpit and said, 'Off you go, on your own, but bring it back in one piece'. After such a display of confidence in me, I taxied out, carefully turned into the wind and took off. The weather was favourable. I flew around for a short time and then approached for my first solo landing. I then did two more take-offs and landings. A bit cheeky.

I was then waved in by the CGE. As I approached the tarmac I noticed Ivor was sitting in the driving seat of the fire engine. When I switched off the aircraft engine, I heard the engine of the fire truck running. All was ready for a Dalton-Morgan prang. As I got out of the cockpit I was greeted by the CGE who said, 'Good for you, you brought it back in one piece. Otherwise you would have to answer to me m'boy, it's my baby'. The owner, CGE and Ivor then took me over to the clubhouse for a celebration drink of champagne. It was a great moment for me.

For the remainder of the few months before I was called forward to the RAF I worked in the hangar with Ivor under the stern but friendly eye of the CGE. I enjoyed occasional flights in the 504K and fairly regular test flights in the Moths with Mr Pope the flying instructor. These were happy days and I learnt a lot.

CHAPTER TWO

Flying Training

I N NOVEMBER 1934, after the months of waiting somewhat anxiously, I received notice to proceed to Bristol-Filton airfield for *ab initio* training for the RAF. Eight pupil pilots were billeted in a house just outside the airfield. We all slept in a dormitory that reminded some of us of school days. The flying training was organised by the then Bristol Aeroplane Company under contract to the Air Ministry.

My instructor was Mr Palmer. He had been a Sergeant Pilot in the RAF. He was an excellent instructor, no nonsense, but friendly and encouraging. While noting my limited flying experience, he put me properly through the *ab initio* flying programme. I had been well prepared by Mr Palmer for my first solo cross-country flight. At the end of each of my training flights he would ask me to point out landmarks and the direction of Filton airfield from our position. On my first solo cross-country I was about three miles north of the track on arrival at Abingdon. After refuelling, I had a satisfactory return flight to Filton in good flying conditions.

After about two months at Filton, with the *ab initio* flying programme completed satisfactory, we pupil pilots reported to RAF Uxbridge. This was for induction into the RAF to learn service protocol, Officers Mess etiquette and Officer relationships with other ranks. Some of this was familiar to those of us who had been in the Officers Training Corps at school.

We started off with squad drill for all of us. Then in turn we moved into the drilling of the squad, learning the commands and the correct time to give them. We were not allowed to play body-contact games (e.g., rugby and football) in case of injury, which could affect future flying training. We were, for example, permitted to play volleyball, badminton and tennis. Daily physical exercise at 0600 hrs and cross-country runs kept us fit.

Interspersed with squad drills, physical training and lectures, we were distributed among the London Military tailors for the fitting and provision of our initial outfit of uniforms. Thereafter we would receive an allowance of £50 per year (at that time) towards the maintenance and replacement of uniforms.

The induction process lasted about six weeks. We were then posted to a Service Flying Training School at Wittering. Here flying training continued on service types of aircraft (e.g., Hawker Hart). We learned how to use the aircraft for military purposes and the general tactics to be employed. Our ground syllabus included lectures on aerial gunnery, bombs and bombing, aerial photography and reconnaissance.

Guns and bombs were taken apart and reassembled. Cameras were loaded with film and mounted in the aircraft. Each pupil pilot then undertook precision aerial reconnaissance photographic runs.

Towards the end of the flying training curriculum, about one month was spent at a bombing and gunnery practice camp at Sutton Bridge on the East Coast. All pupils fired guns against a towed banner and against ground targets. Some dive-bombed ground targets and a few did level bombing.

Returning to the aircraft one day, after firing against a towed aerial target, my engine stopped and the propeller shuddered to a halt. I put my forced landing training into effect and looked around for a likely spot to land. I saw the airfield and considered I may make it. I put the aircraft into a normal glide and approached the airfield, hoping no one would fault my approach and landing. I landed successfully, got out of the aircraft and awaited the approach of the fire truck, ambulance and other vehicles.

After looking around the aircraft, one of our Flight Sergeants climbed into the cockpit and had a look around. After climbing down, he came towards me and said 'I think,

Sir, you forgot to switch over your gravity tank to main tank after take-off'. This was normal practice on the type of aircraft. The Flight Sergeant and I then proceeded to the Flight Commander's Office. After learning my story and the technical explanation of the Flight Sergeant, the Flight Commander first congratulated me on a successful forced landing. He then said, 'Now get your parachute on and run around the perimeter of the airfield twice. I shall be watching you. After that, I am sure you will not forget to switch over tanks again'. With those words ringing in my ears I set off on my hike carrying our 90lb parachute. On my return to Wittering, my flying instructor said, 'He had heard of the incident and considered it had been properly dealt with and that was the end of the matter'.

While at Wittering, Fred Rosier (later Air Chief Marshal Rosier) and P R 'Johnny' Walker (later Group Captain Walker) and I became firm friends. I had the car and used to take Fred to see his girlfriend (the now Lady Hetty) a very dear lady. Some forty years later Lady Hetty told of how her landlady used to complain of the mess I made in her garden while having something to eat waiting for Fred.

The remainder of my flying training course at Wittering was completed without incident. I had been given to understand that I would be posted to a fighter squadron along with my friends Fred and Johnny. Alas, no. I was sent on a short engineering course that included a spell at the Whitehead torpedo factory at Weymouth. There I had torpedo maintenance and preparation for flight. I was then put on a torpedo dropping course followed by deck landing training. That ended at sea in the aircraft carrier HMS *Furious*. My short tour with the Fleet Air Arm ended as a deck-landing instructor at Gosport. This was done in a Tutor aircraft. The pupil flew under the hood with an instructor/safety pilot in the second cockpit. Only the basic instruments for flying were available – air speed indicator, altimeter, turn and bank indicator and, of course, the compass. The course included take-offs and approaches to land and triangular cross-country fights, all under the hood.

Thereafter, whenever practicable, I maintained myself in

instrument flying practice. Years later, when they were introduced, I obtained my green ticket that permitted me to fly under minimum meteorological flying conditions. As a squadron commander and wing leader this was a great confidence booster.

CHAPTER THREE

Pre-War Years in the RAF

AFTER completing the instrument flying course I was posted to No. 22 Torpedo-Bomber Squadron in Fife, Scotland. The aerodrome at Donibristle, as they were called in those pre-war days, was small, grass covered and undulating. The Officer's Mess was on a hill on the north side of the aerodrome. When the wind blew 25-30 knots from the north, aircraft took-off and landed up the hill and almost ended up close to the door of the mess, sometimes too close. Fortunately the prevailing winds were westerly and southerly.

On arrival at the Squadron I was allocated to the duties of squadron adjutant, of which I knew little or nothing. Fortunately, I had an Orderly Room Corporal who was competent and helpful. The Commanding Officer soon made me aware of what he expected of me. The Station Engineer Officer acquainted me with my responsibilities for the maintenance and preparation for flight of torpedoes and their recovery from the sea after drops.

The above duties seemed to be mutually exclusive. However, I managed them with the assistance of a tolerant Commanding Officer, a good Orderly Room Corporal and efficient and friendly Station Engineer and a competent Flight Sergeant in the torpedo workshop. They held my hand until I could walk alone.

The other pilots were rotated through ground duties such as Navigation Officer, Parachute Officer, Stores Officer and Duty Pilot. On Saturday and Monday mornings we sprog pilots all worked in the hangar alongside the airmen and aircraft maintenance. This was good for *esprit de corps* and pilots and ground crews getting to know each other.

Adjutant duties in particular did interfere to some extent with my flying. I kept my eye on the pilots' monthly flying hours tables in the Flight Commander's office. I also showed up in his office occasionally if I noticed my hours were lagging. For flying I was allocated to 'B' flight. The Flight Commander was Flight Lieutenant Griffiths. He, quite rightly, would not stand any nonsense. He was tough, fair, likeable and respected. He would have been in his thirties, like his peers in those days.

At this time, the aircraft used for the carriage and delivery of the torpedo was the Vickers Wildebeest. This was a single engine plane, 840-hp radial engine, and two-blade propeller. Maximum speed was about 110mph. It carried a pilot, rear-seat air gunner/wireless operator and one torpedo. The pilot had one fixed gun firing through the propeller with synchronising constantenesco gears. The rear gunner had a single gun that commanded a restricted firing arc on each side and above and below the aircraft.

As regards the torpedoes my excellent Flight Sergeant supervised workshop activity. With him, I ensured the required number of dummy and live running torpedoes were ready for a dropping session. We also supervised loading on to the aircraft and testing and arming of the compressed air motors of the live runners. The dummy torpedo was simply a piece of iron shaped like a live torpedo and positively buoyed to facilitate recovery after dropping. The live torpedo was complete for running against target except for a warhead and buoyed positively for recovery.

The dummy torpedoes were for pilots to learn and practice the correct dropping height (23-30ft). When a pilot achieved consistent dropping proficiency, he proceeded to live drops. If dropped correctly a live torpedo would run the correct range and surface at the end of the run for recovery and servicing for future runs. Dropped too low, it would stave in the underside of a fabric-covered aircraft. If a live torpedo was dropped too high it usually resulted in no run and sometimes loss of the torpedo.

When the Royal Navy had ships conveniently at sea, live drops were carried out against such ships as targets with the co-operation of the RN. This provided pilot training in dropping, ranging to the target and aiming off to allow ship speed. For all drops a recovery tender was provided, sometimes two. The tender(s) carried the torpedo recovery team and Flight Commanders or experienced pilots deputised to assess each drop. Tactical approaches and attacks against ships by flight and squadron were also practised.

There were, of course, other forms of flying training, for example, navigation exercises and formation flying. A favourite of our Flight Commander was to lead my friend Pilot Officer Tennant and myself in 'Vic' formation, flying in cloud. This kept us in instrument flying practice and improved our formation flying and confidence. We stuck close to him in cloud. There was also bombing and gunnery at the annual practice camps. This was highly competitive. We competed against other squadrons. One year I was selected to represent Coastal Command in a high dive-bombing competition at the annual RAF air show at Hendon. I was awarded a silver tankard.

From time to time the squadron would fly to a base in the south to participate in formal inter-service exercises. As squadron adjutant I would be responsible for the administration during such moves, particularly for the welfare of the airmen.

Life for a 'sprog' pilot in a squadron in those pre-war years in the thirties was pleasant. There were plenty of flying and other interesting tasks to which we had to turn a hand from time to time. Presumably this was why aircrew became known at that time as the General Duties Branch. Occasionally we would be permitted to take an aircraft away for a long weekend, this had to be approved by the Flight Commander and the Squadron Commanding Officer, including flight plan and the adequacy of the facilities at the destination airfield. The minimum meteorological for such flights was also prescribed according to the pilots experience and perceived skill.

At that time, 1935, the Forth railway bridge was the only bridge across the Firth. It was not far from Donibristle. It was forbidden to fly under the bridge. Nevertheless, from time to time, pilots had attempted it successfully. One day when I was airborne alone, I thought I would make an attempt to fly under the bridge. The visibility was good and winds were light. There was no shipping in the vicinity, no trains on the bridge and no other aircraft around. I dropped down to sea level and lined up to fly through the centre span.

I knew the measurements of the bridge centre span and height from sea level to the bridge platform and, of course, the wingspan of my aircraft. My aircraft would go through the centre span easily. Nevertheless, as I approached near to the bridge and, concentrating on maintaining my height above sea level and my track through the centre of the span, the bridge looked formidable and menacing. It was too late to turn away. In the next two or three seconds I was through. I turned sharply to port, climbed away and hoped I had not been seen. Only then did I notice the painters on the southern end of the bridge. They gave me what appeared to be a friendly wave, as I climbed away. I said nothing of my act of bravado on my return to the airfield, in the pilots' room or in the mess. I hoped I had got away with it.

However, I did receive a fright. A day or so later, we heard in the Mess that a naval officer pilot had been spotted as he flew under the bridge. He was being court-martialled. I do not think anyone in the squadron made an attempt for a long time after this incident.

Sometime after the above incident had faded, another young officer, Pilot Officer Charles Lester and myself, were flying south led by Flight Lieutenant Jock Campbell, a good type. He would soon be promoted to command a squadron. Our planned re-fuelling stop was RAF Grantham. As we approached Grantham it was 'soaked-in'. That is, weather conditions at the airfield would prevent us landing. We were low on fuel. Our leader turned north, we closed formation on him, he called on the intercom that he would look for a forced landing field and that we were to follow him in.

He found a suitable field and made a successful approach and landing. It was not a long field but clearly big enough with a careful approach. My turn was next. I circled the field and after Flight Lieutenant Campbell had taxied to one side of the field I made my approach and landed successfully. I got out of the cockpit, walked over and stood with our leader to watch Charles approach and land. His first attempt was too fast over the hedge; he opened the throttle and went round again. His second attempt looked better but he was still a little fast over the hedge. He touched down too far down the field and ended up in the hedge.

Flight Lieutenant Campbell and I ran over to Charles' aircraft as he climbed out of his cockpit. Naturally, he was unhappy. We all walked around and inspected Charles' aircraft for damage, there appeared to be none. The overshoot into the hedge had been slow, the hedge had stopped the propeller, but it seemed undamaged. By this time the farmer and two of his workers appeared on the scene. They helped us push Charles' aircraft near the other two at the side of the field where we had landed.

Flight Lieutenant Campbell explained to the farmer the reason for our precautionary landings and that we would be there overnight. We were about ten miles north of RAF Grantham. The farmer invited us up to his home. Flight Lieutenant Campbell went on with the farmer to use his telephone to inform Grantham of the situation and arrange for guarding assistance for the aircraft. Flight Lieutenant Campbell spoke to the Duty Officer at Grantham. He explained the situation and said we would fly into Grantham on the morrow, re-fuel and continue our fight south. At his request, overnight guards for the aircraft would be sent out and in the morning give assistance to start up the aircraft.

In the meantime, Charles and I got out the cockpit covers and pickets to tie down the lower wings and tail plane of each aircraft against the possibility of high winds. Charles then followed up to the farmer's house, while I took first watch to guard the aircraft. The farmer's three young children then arrived to be shown over the aircraft. This was an interesting diversion for me, during my watch. After some two/three hours Charles arrived back with two airmen of the first watch complete with flasks of hot tea and sandwiches provided by the farmer's wife.

Leaving Charles and the two airmen on watch I proceeded

to the farmhouse. Here I was provided with bacon, eggs and tea by the kindly farmer's wife. Charles and I took it in turns to be with the guards on duty as they changed over throughout the night. We spent a pleasant evening chatting with the farmer and his family. They were excited to have us there. We partook of the excellent homemade wine. During the evening Flight Lieutenant Campbell explained to the farmer how he could be recompensed for his help and hospitality. Later we all settled down, pilots and off duty guards on comfortable chairs and sofas to sleep. The only movement was at the changing of the guard. Outside it was a cloudy and cold spring night.

Early next morning we were awakened with cups of tea. Later we were provided with an excellent breakfast. Flight Lieutenant Campbell, myself, the off duty guards and the family then proceeded down to the aircraft. Charles and his watch then went up to the house for breakfast. At the aircraft we were joined by mechanics, who had been sent to help us start the engines. We were also joined by farm workers and curious bystanders. Helped by the mechanics we stowed the cockpit covers and pickets and made the aircraft ready to start. By this time Charles had returned from the farmhouse. We thanked the farmer and his family and bid them farewell, we thanked the airmen for their help and climbed aboard our aircraft. We started up the engines and after warming up we taxied to the other end of the field. We took off singly, formed up in a close 'Vic' and made a farewell run over the field. We then headed for Grantham where the weather had cleared. After re-fuelling we flew on our way to our destination in the south.

While I was at Donibristle I became friendly with Flying Officer Dick Beauman. We had common interests, one being sand-yachting. When the Squadron moved to Thorney Island, we used to go up to London where we would stay with his mother at her apartment in Paddington. Together we would sample what London had to offer. However, Dick would sometimes go off to see his girlfriend, a very lovely girl, leaving me to my own devices. Instead of London we would sometimes motor down to Woolacombe in North Devon and really enjoy sand yachting on what was then a very quiet beach. We would stay in the Woolacombe Sands Hotel with the hospitality of the manager who was a friend of Dick and his mother. On one occasion Dick confided in me that he thought his girlfriend was pregnant. He was agonizing over this fact until, a short time after being told, he received a telegram from his girlfriend when we were both staying for the weekend at Woolacombe. The cryptic note read ... 'Red Sails in the Sunset'.

Sometime after the forced landing episode, the squadron was moved to a base on the south coast of England. Shortly afterwards I was posted to a desk job at Air Ministry, London. Not before Harry Tennant, Tony Hibberd and myself had made contact with our friends of flying training days – Fred Rosier and Peter (Johnny) Walker at a neighbouring fighter station. This gave us an opportunity to fly their Hawker Fury Fighters. This of course left us envious.

CHAPTER FOUR

A Stint at the Air Ministry

IN 1937 a new policy had been agreed between the
Admiralty and Air Ministry. This had been approved by the
Government of the day. In the future the Royal Navy would
not only be responsible for the aircraft carriers and their
operation as hitherto, but would take over from the RAF
responsibility for the provision, manning and maintenance of
Fleet Air Arm (FAA) aircraft. The RAF would continue to
provide support as necessary until naval manning of the FAA
had built up. This would include the flying training of naval
aircrew.

My duties at the Air Ministry and those of my naval
counterpart involved the overall supervision of the flying
training of naval aircrew to replace RAF aircrew doing a tour
of duty in the FAA. Also, the transfer of aircraft and
associated equipment from an RAF inventory to a Naval
inventory. My first Royal Navy counterpart was much senior
to me and had undoubtedly participated in the policy
discussions. Later he became Captain of the aircraft carrier
HMS *Ark Royal*, where he served with great distinction.
When he went back to sea he was replaced by Lieutenant
Commander Williamson, who was later killed in the
Swordfish torpedo bomber raid on the Italian fleet in Taranto
harbour. I was a dogsbody acting Flight Lieutenant who
watched over the flying training of naval aircrew and
maintained significant equipment from RAF inventory to
naval inventories.

Both those naval officers were a pleasure to work with.
Our duties involved much liaison between Air Ministry,

Admiral House and the Admiralty. Fortunately there was also some flying. We made frequent visits to the two flying schools at Peterborough and Netheravon where naval aircrew pilots for the Fleet Air Arm (FAA) were being trained. I did the piloting in a small communications aircraft of the Air Ministry Flight at Hendon.

The work bored all three of us, but we knew it had to be done. It was early 1940, and we were now at war. Commander Atkinson was the first out; he went back to sea, which is what he wanted. I felt it was my turn next. I explained to Lieutenant Commander Williamson my work was virtually finished and would he mind if I went to see my Director about getting back to flying. He had no objection and said he would support my request if necessary.

I then sought an interview with my Director who was the Director of Training. He was the most senior officer I had to face up to since my original interview. I was shown into his office. He was seated at his desk with a civilian suited person seated nearby. 'Now Dalton-Morgan, what do you want?' I explained that my task at Air Ministry was virtually finished and that I wished to return to flying duties, preferably on active service in fighters. I understood there was a shortage of fighter pilots with experience. I said I had about five hours flying experience on Hurricanes (which was not strictly true) but I thought it would help. I added that Lieutenant Commander Williamson was willing to release me. The Director said, 'I admire your spirit Dalton-Morgan. I will do all I can to help you'. I thanked him and left.

A few days later I received a posting to a refresher unit. I thanked Lieutenant Commander Williamson and my Director, said *adieu* and headed north to RAF Sutton Bridge to fly. Here there were a few young pilots like myself who were undergoing refresher flying after ground jobs. I fell into the capable and experienced hands of Flight Sergeant Soper, ex No. 1 Squadron. I had met him briefly previously at RAF Tangmere. He was being rested after the hectic time No. 1 squadron experienced in France, where he had shot down eight German aircraft, plus four more shared. He was killed on the 5th December, 1941, as a Squadon Leader with the

Distinguished Flying Medal (DFM) and the Distinguished Flying Cross (DFC).

After a few hours converting to the Gladiator and Hurricane I commenced serious tactical flying with Sergeant Soper. I was an eager pupil and Soper was willing to impart all he had learnt in combat with the *Luftwaffe*. Flight Sergeant Soper had already learnt that flying as a section of three, as we did, was perilous for No. 3. The *Luftwaffe* flew as two sections of two in finger four formations.

One day, after flying around the cumulus clouds trying to get on each other's tail, we landed. Over a mug of tea he told me I was posted to No. 43 Squadron, Tangmere. The two of us had a quiet celebration that night. I have always felt that Fight Sergeant Soper had something to do with my posting to one of the old famous squadrons. Anyway, for all that he showed me I will always be grateful.

CHAPTER FIVE

43 Squadron

O N ARRIVAL at Tangmere in late May 1940 I reported to the Adjutant of 43 Squadron, one Stewart Carey, of which more later. I cannot remember our conversation except that it was friendly and helpful. He had already arranged for my room in the mess. He then wheeled me in to meet the Commanding Officer of 43 Squadron, Squadron Leader George Lott. Again I was greeted and welcomed in a most friendly manner. The CO told me I was to be 'B' Flight Commander and gave me a run down on the pilots and current operations situations. We then went off to the 'B' Flight dispersal area to meet the pilots, my Flight Sergeant to be, Flight Sergeant Yates, a loyal, stalwart and the airmen of the flight. We then went off to lunch where I met 'A' Flight Commander Peter Townsend and the other pilots. On that day the Squadron was at operational state – 'released from operations'.

The next day I was thrown in at the deep end. 'A' Flight came to state 'readiness' at dawn, that is at dispersal but awaiting the order from sector operations to 'scramble' (take-off). The only higher order of readiness was sitting in the cockpit at 'cockpit readiness'. 'B' Flight was to go to France to support the French Air Force for midday returning to home at last light. The two flights alternated on this arrangement for the short time it lasted. The Prime Minister had wished to send more squadrons to France to support the French, however, Commander-in-Chief Fighter Command, Sir Hugh Dowding, had said if more squadrons were sent to France he could not be responsible for the air defence of the UK. Hence the compromise to send a few flights from different squadrons to France for one-day detachments only.

'B' Flight did three such temporary detachments from base at Tangmere. On the third we were warned by telephone that *Wehrmacht* troops were approaching the airfield. We looked outside the tent. Sure enough, we could see *Wehrmacht* motorcyclists, staff cars and what looked like troop trucks in the distance. I ordered the 'scramble' for return to the UK. The first two sections of two Hurricanes took off to attack the German column.

My No. 2 and I remained last to see our ground troops off in the deHavilland Dragon. We then taxied out to take-off. A truck carrying some French troops deliberately blocked our way. I got out of the cockpit and told the French NCO to get his truck out of the way and, when he told me not to take off, I threatened him with my revolver. By this time my No. 2 was at my side with his revolver pointed at the troops in the truck, who did not appear to be armed. The NCO still refused to move the truck, so I shot him. There was too much at stake. The truck was moved away smartly and my No. 2 and I climbed into our aircraft and took off. We joined up with the other four Hurricanes and continued attacks on the German column. The tanks, of course, were too much for our .303 bullets. Without loss we headed back to base at Tangmere for a cup of tea on landing and a beer in the mess. I had been blooded to some extent.

During the next few weeks, before the start of the Battle of Britain proper (official dates 10th July-October 1940), the Squadron was involved in air protection of shipping convoys still using the English Channel, the interception of single and small numbers of *Luftwaffe* aircraft and combat training of new pilots. We also participated in providing air cover over the Dunkirk beaches and the 'little ships' as they bravely plied to and fro across the Channel to rescue some 350,000 of the British Expeditionary Force.

During this period I made my first claim against the *Luftwaffe*. On the 3rd July, 1940, I intercepted a Dornier Do17 about to escape across the Channel. It may have been the Do17 that had earlier attacked an *ab initio* flying

TDM when Wing Leader at Ibsley

Pilots of 43 Squadron during the Battle of Britain.

43 Squadron *left to right*, Upton, Mills, (?), Lott, Carey, Reynell, (?), (?), Kilmartin, (?). *(via Bill Littlemore)*

Hurricanes of 43 Squadron at Tangmere, 1940. *(via Bill Littlemore)*

Ju 88 after a neat belly landing.

A painting of a 43 Squadron Hurricane dealing with a Ju 88.
(via Bill Littlemore)

The deadly 88 Flak guns. *(Bundesarchiv)*

A series of five photographs showing 24 Luftwaffe bombers, of III./KG 51, attacking RAF Warmwell on 25 August, 1940.

Fw 190s in France *(Bundesarchiv)*

Ju 88s in flight

TDM with the unofficial 'Fighting Cock' emblem *(via Bill Littlemore)*

training school near Maidenhead. I made three attacks on the aircraft. The Do17 escaped into cloud before I could close to effective range on the first two attacks. On the third attack I was able to close to 200 yards before he escaped into cloud again. I scored hits on the starboard mainplane and engine. I received no return fire and assumed the gunman had become a casualty. It finally disappeared into a cloud at 800ft that extended right across the Channel. I was awarded a 'damaged' for this claim.

In the early days after I joined 43 Squadron most of our work was convoy patrols and interception of Heinkel He111 bomber raids, escorted by Messerschmitt Bf109 against shipping convoys. Eventually, it became too hazardous for our shipping to use the English Channel. They started to make greater use of the West Coast ports.

The *Luftwaffe* effort against the convoys had also been expensive but the Channel was cleared of British and Allied shipping. It had now to turn its main effort to the second phase of its operations preceding the invasion of Britain. This was the defeat of the RAF fighter force. This started with attempts to neutralise our radar stations along the South Coast. This was followed up with bombing attacks on our fighter airfields, south and west of London. These were destroyed but were rapidly repaired. I was in sick quarters when our own base at Tangmere was hit. But we were able to remain operational. The *Stuka* – Junkers Ju87 – was withdrawn from operations towards the end of this phase.

It was now well into August 1940. The planned invasion date in September was now approaching. The *Luftwaffe* had now to turn its attention to the third phase of its pre-invasion plan of its operation with RAF still undefeated and still changing. The third phase was the destruction of support facilities, e.g., fuel, food and ammunition for the British defence forces. Opposing the invasion the RAF attrition against the *Luftwaffe* day operations was such that the *Luftwaffe* was forced to turn to night bombing operations.

The above is what is generally considered to be the Battle of Britain. Historians have subsequently divided the battle into three or four phases with slightly differing dates. However, what is generally agreed is that the battle took place between the 10th July-30th October 1940 with the exception of the *Luftwaffe* who did not recognise definite dates.

At this time in June 1940 the *Luftwaffe* was redeploying its squadrons in France, Belgium, the Netherlands and Norway in preparation for the assault on the UK. Its efforts were mainly air reconnaissance of sensitive targets in the British war economy and relatively small bomber raids escorted by fighters to test our reactions. Our integrated air defence system, comprising the early warning radar and co-ordinated fighter and AR defences and Observer Corps land tracking system were being exercised under real war conditions.

In these combats where usually we were so heavily outnumbered it occurred to me that we could complete attacks on the enemy bombers before the enemy fighters found us. At the time I did not think I would survive. I was determined to take as many of the enemy with me as possible. To die in battle was a good way to go. Here I am, writing about it years later.

However, we had some advantages. First, we were fighting over our own country. If we fell to the enemy but survived we lived to fight another day. When *Luftwaffe* aircrew fell to us over the United Kingdom he died or was taken prisoner of war. Secondly, we had radar, the use of which meant we held a technical advantage over the enemy in 1940. The early development had been in its use for defence. It:

a. gave us early warning of enemy aircraft assembling and forming up over northern France, likely intentions and direction of attack

b. enabled our enemy aircraft interception line to be pushed out over the Channel

c. allowed our fighters to be held on the ground until enemy intentions became clear

d. enabled our fighters to be directed into the best possible tactical position for attack

At the outset of the Battle the *Luftwaffe* had more tactical combat experience than us. It had participated in the Spanish war and flew against the Czech and Polish airforces. However, we learned quickly but at some cost, particularly as regards tactical combat formations. The calibre and skill of *Luftwaffe* and RAF fighter pilots seemed comparable.

During late June 1940 and early July the *Luftwaffe* endeavoured to draw Fighter Command fighters into a decisive battle for air superiority. It carried out Bf109 fighter sweeps mainly over south east England and the English Channel. Fighter Command of course reacted. From a German point of view, this phase of the Battle was indecisive. The integrated resources of fighters, radar and Observer Corps enabled the inferior numbers of RAF fighters to be used economically and with advantage. The radar provided early warning of a threat, direction and height information and some indication of numbers. It also enabled early interception to be extended over the English Channel. The Observer Corps provided tracking information of enemy aircraft overland. The radar and overland tracking information was transmitted to a Sector Control where it was used to give the RAF fighters direction and height information with advantage and an indication of the size of the enemy threat.

This fighter *versus* fighter phase enabled the *Luftwaffe* pilots and ourselves to test and check the performance of our respective aircraft in combat. The Bf109 could fly higher than the Hurricane. However, the latter could turn inside the former in combat. This was a useful superiority in combat. Similarly, the Spitfire could turn inside the Bf109 and had a slightly superior speed and altitude performance. In the Battle of Britain some of the Bf109s were equipped with a 20mm canon, firing through the nose and two machine guns. The Hurricanes and Spitfires carried eight machine guns, four in each wing. The struggle for superior fighter performance between RAF and *Luftwaffe* alternated throughout the war. The fighting and flying ability of RAF and *Luftwaffe* fighter pilots were generally similar.

The *Luftwaffe* pilots had fought their way across Europe and had gained tactical and combat experience. At the outset of the Battle of Britain they were superior to us. However, we learnt quickly with experience. Our basic 'Vics' of three were swapped in favour of sections of four made up of sub-sections of two. These were separated by distances that gave them adequate tactical manoeuvrability and at the same time maintaining unit cohesion.

In addition to participating in the fighter versus fighter phase, 43 Squadron also participated in providing air cover over the Dunkirk beaches and the 'little ships' as they plied bravely to and fro across the Channel in the final phase of the rescue of some 350,000 men of the British Expeditionary Force of some 500,000 men that were sent to France to assist the French in the defence of Western Europe.

At one time in July and August 1940 there were up to nine convoys between the straits of Dover and the Western end of the Channel near the Lizard. These convoys were provided with air cover from fighter squadrons at Portsmouth and Exeter in the West, Tangmere (including 43 Squadron) in the centre and the squadrons from bases around London in the East-Thames estuary and straits of Dover. Often the Tangmere squadrons were required to fly eighty miles East to reinforce the London squadrons.

As an outcome of this phase in *Luftwaffe* air operations, our merchant shipping became restricted to the West Coast ports of the British Isles. The Royal Navy continued to operate in the English Channel with flight support.

On the 9th July, 1940, our excellent Commanding Officer, Squadron Leader George Lott, was shot down by return fire from a Me110 of III./ZG26. The windscreen of his Hurricane was shattered and splinters entered his right eye. He baled out at 700ft. He lost the sight of his right eye that ended his operational career. He eventually retired from the RAF as an Air Vice-Marshal with a CB, CBE, DSO and DFC. He was succeeded in 43 Squadron by Squadron Leader Badger, an excellent officer and Commander whom

I had known previously.

Sometimes the *Luftwaffe* bombers would appear over their target with no fighter support. Other bombers would appear with unusually large fighter support. From German reports it appears this was caused by poor *Luftwaffe* fighter/bomber rendezvous over the belated rendezvous point on the French coast. Sometimes the bombers were late or would meet and join up with one group of bombers and unknowingly leave another without any fighter support, usually with disastrous results for the unescorted bombers.

After denying the use of the English Channel to most Merchant Shipping supporting the British Isles, the *Luftwaffe* turned its attention to the RAF fighter system. This included bombing and fighter strikes on some of our radar early warning stations and RAF fighter airfields in the South. The latter included aircraft on the ground as well as in the air and fighter support facilities. After these attacks the *Luftwaffe* headquarters of *Generaloberst* Kesselring prematurely wrote off all the fighter units on the airfields attacked, despite the protestations of fighter leaders Galland and Mölders. These officers were right. Damage was caused but not complete destruction. All airfields and units attacked survived to fight the *Luftwaffe* again.

After the attacks on radars and airfields, the Ju87 dive-bomber formations were withdrawn from the West. They were too vulnerable and easy targets for our Hurricanes and Spitfires. The loss rate was too high. Soon afterwards the Messerschmitt Me110, a twin-engine fighter, was also withdrawn, it was no match for the Hurricanes and Spitfires. It was converted to a night-fighter role to deal with our expanding night bomber force.

After the attacks on airfields the *Luftwaffe* turned its main bombing effort onto what we would call strategic targets, e.g., aircraft production, fuel production, port facilities and communications etc. some of these targets required relatively deep penetration. The bombers and fighter support were subject to Fighter Command attacks during penetration and withdrawal. These raids became too expensive in daylight. The Battle of Britain was virtually

over. The planned invasion of Britain in September had
been abandoned. In October 1940 the *Luftwaffe* started to
turn to night bombing. The 'Knickenbeam' was introduced
to improve bombing accuracy. These were laid on to
intercept over the target. The bombers then flew one of the
beams to the interception point where bombs were
dropped.

On 12th July the weather was indifferent with rain in
most places. As Commander of 'B' Flight I normally led
'blue' section. At 1430 hours we were scrambled to
intercept a Heinkel He111 over Southampton flying at
8,000ft.

I saw the 'bandit' on the port side below me at 8,000ft. I
led 'Blue' Section into attack. I turned onto his tail and went
in for the first attack. I opened fire at 200yds and closed to
100yds. During this burst the starboard wing broke up and
the engine blew up. I was enveloped in smoke and fragments
for about three seconds. I broke away and followed him
through cloud. I made a second attack after 'Blue' section
and opened fire at 200yds and closed to 100yds to take out
or leave the aircraft. This time fragments and black smoke
came from the port engine. The bandit then commenced to
glide towards the ground. I followed him down. He selected
a field four miles north of Fort Nelson and landed in a
northerly direction and ended up in a hedge near a
farmhouse. No one was seen to bale out. I was fired on by
the air gunner and was hit in the plane.

Pilot Officer Gorrie, my 'Blue 2', also took part in this
attack. He reported in his Combat Report, 'the starboard
engine was seen to blow up following "Blue 1" attack'.
When 'Blue 1' broke away I went in and followed with two
short bursts before the Heinkel dived away into cloud.

The Heinkel crashed near the Horse and Jockey Public
House at Hipley. The landlord saw the bomber coming
down and armed himself with his son's toy pistol.
Fortunately his bluff was never called. Of the crew of five,
Oberleutnant Kleinhanns was killed. *Feldwebel* John Mohn,
Feldwebel Heinz Knecht, *Oberfeldwebel* P Muller, and
Feldwebel H Kalina, became prisoners of war. The Heinkel

belonged to Stab./KG55.

The *Luftwaffe* fighters sometimes had problems meeting up with their bomber formations at the selected rendezvous points on the French coast. This caused some trouble between the fighter and bomber leaders. Sometimes the bombers were late, on other occasions all the fighters would meet and join up with one group of bombers and leave another without any fighter support, usually with disastrous results for the bombers.

Another problem causing trouble between the *Luftwaffe* fighters and bomber leaders was the latter's insistence that the close escort fighters remain rigidly close to the bombers. This did not allow the fighters sufficient space for combat manoeuvrability. Galland and Mölders, two of the fighter leaders, protested. They wanted the close escort fighters to be moved out to a distance from the bombers, where they could deal more effectively with any aircraft attempting to attack the bombers. However, the Air Fleet Commanders, *Generaloberst* Kesselring and *Generaloberst* Sperrle supported the bomber leaders.

To provide some withdrawal support for their returning bombers, the *Luftwaffe* sometimes provided fighters, at or near the French coast, to pick up returning bombers and escort them to their planes. This was to provide a counter to some of the RAF fighters that would follow and attack the *Luftwaffe* bombers returning across the Channel to their bases.

During the Battle of Britain the *Luftwaffe* fighters were generally required to fly three different types of mission. One day they would fly support missions for Air/Sea rescue units. On the second day they would provide bomber support to the UK targets. On the third day they would provide withdrawal support for the bombers at the French coast as indicated above.

It was during the *Luftwaffe* operations outlined above that we quickly learnt from them how out of date our fighter battle formations were. We quickly adopted the basic subsection of two fighters and sections of four, spread some 300 metres apart, as a basic battle formation. This contributed to a reduction in our loss rate and to the RAF fighter successes against the *Luftwaffe* bombers and fighters.

On the 13th July 'Blue' section was at cockpit readiness – sitting in the cockpit, strapped up and ready to scramble, except for engine start. Our phone monitor came running out of the dispersal hut and gave us the scramble sign. As soon as we were airborne Tangmere Sector Control gave us the vector to steer to interrupt a suspect 'bandit', as the enemy aircraft were known. Radar reported it at clouds (altitude) 150ft. We continued on an intercepting vector as given by Sector Control. We eventually saw a Ju88 flying south and out of cumulus cloud south of the Isle of Wight. I gave the 'tally ho' and, in formation, we closed to attack. By this time we were well over the Channel and beyond the ten-mile limit RAF fighter pilots were not supposed to exceed at that time.

There appeared to be no other enemy aircraft in the vicinity. As we came within firing range, I opened fire and continued to attack with several short bursts. There was no return fire. After two or three attacks, one engine, I forget which, caught fire, the other was smoking. The Ju88 was now descending rapidly, seemingly under control. We made one last attack to ensure the Ju88 would not make land. It eventually ditched in the sea off the French coast. Two airmen got out of the aircraft into a circular dinghy. We orbited the scene until the Ju88 sank and then returned to base. We reported the incident and had a cup of tea while our aircraft were re-armed and re-fuelled and returned to readiness.

Many years later I learned the aircraft was from 6./KG51. Of the crew, *Oberleutnant* Fritz Kesper was killed and three others were missing.

By this time the *Luftwaffe* had moved its bombers, He111, Ju88, Do17 and Do215 and Ju87 dive-bombers into bases in northern France, the Netherlands and Norway ready for the assault on the UK. Now that bombers were available the next phase on the German overall plan for the invasion of the UK was to deny the use of the English Channel to the Royal Navy and to merchant shipping proceeding to and from the London ports and East Coast ports.

Fighter command was soon maintaining standing patrols over shipping in the Channel. Normally, these patrols were small, two to four aircraft. However, as soon as our radar reported the approach of an enemy bomber force, the RAF standing patrols were reinforced by sufficient fighters to deal with the bombers and distract the supporting *Luftwaffe* fighters.

The weather continued fine day after day during that 1940 summer and of course favoured the *Luftwaffe* bombers and kept our RAF fighters busy. Between sorties we virtually lived at dispersal. The *Luftwaffe* operations were falling into a general pattern. Early morning weather and target recces, then a morning bomber raid followed by an afternoon raid. Our primary task was to destroy as many bombers as possible before they reached the target and break up their formations and continue to attack them as they withdrew. Some of our fighters of course had to be diverted to deal with the *Luftwaffe* fighters supporting the bombers. We were now required to fly in sub-sections of two like the *Luftwaffe* fighters. If enabled flexible formation and ensured four sub sections to manoeuvre tactically and look out for each other. I found as a flight commander that a tactical formation of three to four pairs was more effective to handle. Our squadrons detailed for fighter cover would deal with the enemy fighters.

On the 21st July, 1940, approximately 9am three RAF squadrons, including 43 Squadron, intercepted German aircraft over convoy 'Peewit' in the English Channel. My 'Blue' section of six aircraft, at 13,000ft above and behind a large number of Dornier Do17 bombers in waves of eight, stepped up in to the sun with an escort of Bf109s. The enemy aircraft were attacking the convoy from astern. My section climbed and engaged the escort of Bf109s. I received one round in my port headlight. I destroyed one Bf109 that I observed crash into the sea and a second Bf109 damaged. Unfortunately, Pilot Officer de Mancha was killed when he collided with a Bf109.

Most of the engagements with the *Luftwaffe* raids were over Kent and the South East convoys on the English Channel and the approaches to the London targets. The eighty miles flight from Tangmere to the battle area gave us time to change to the altitude and above of the enemy fighter support to the bombers and gave us some advantage. Sometimes it enabled the Bf109s to be diverted from our squadrons attacking the bombers.

The battle formations we had adopted were flexible and easier for sub-sections to manoeuvre tactically and look out for each other. I found as a flight commander that a tactical formation of two pairs was more effective and easier to handle. At this time we were flying three to four sorties a day – sometimes two squadron sorties, sorties by one flight and one or two sorties by two sections of two aircraft. It was only possible to maintain such a flying effort by the unstinting support of our loyal ground crews by day and by night. Each aircraft on the flight line had a ground crew of two and usually the same pilot. With the pilot each formed a team of three to keep the aircraft flying and ready for combat. My ground crew on Hurricane FT-G were Bill Littlemore and Tommy Poole. I cannot speak too highly of their unrelenting efforts and loyalty in keeping my aircraft in fighting trim. I kept in touch with Bill until he died in early 2002, but we both lost contact with Tommy. Our flight line ground crew were also well supported by equally loyal and diligent armament, radio and instrument crews who serviced more than one aircraft.

When an aircraft was taken off the flight line for second or third line maintenance by the hangar maintenance crews, the flight line ground crews would go with the aircraft to the hangar to help and to return the aircraft to the flight line as quickly as possible. This usually meant working through the night. All was organised to maintain a maximum flying effort by our Flight Sergeants, Yates of 'B' Flight and Parker of 'A' Flight, together with the Squadron Engineer Officer. This team spirit was essential to the squadron flying efficiency and *esprit de corps*.

The attacks against the convoys in the English Channel

saw the *Luftwaffe* Ju87 *Stuka* in large formations for the first time. 43 Squadron played a part in destroying the possible threat of these aircraft and their removal from the Western theatre. Prior to this date the Ju87 Stukas had been a main weapon of the German *blitzkrieg* advance across Europe.

The first big *Stuka* attack occurred on 8th August, 1940, when heavy fighting took place over a large convoy CW9, code name 'Peewit'. *Luftflotte* 3 Commander, *Generalfeldmarschall* Kesselring saw it as an opportunity to use the Stukas for precision attack on the ships while the Bf109s would deal with RAF Fighters. The dive-bomber force consisted of Ju87s from *Stuka Geschwaderen* 2, 3 and 77. The fighter escort was provided by Bf109s from *Jagdgeschwader* 27 and a small number of Me110s from V./LG1.

As usual I led 43 Squadron's 'Blue' Section, which comprised myself and Sergeant Hurry. At about 1620 hours and south of the Isle of Wight I engaged a Ju87 that was the nearest of an echelon of five. The Ju87 immediately caught fire and dived into the sea. Sgt Hurry later confirmed this claim. I then tackled the next Ju87 that, after a short burst, turned over emitting black smoke. Then with my section I concentrated on the three remaining Ju87s but was attacked by a Bf109. However, I did a tight turn on to his tail and attacked. He then dived towards the sea and I followed him down. He then turned and climbed up towards me, head on. I engaged him and he then burst into flames and crashed into the sea.

In Francis Mason's excellent book, *Battle over Britain*, he says, 'Flight Lieutenant Thomas Morgan was also well positioned for an attack. It was almost certainly Morgan himself who, attacking the lead formation of escorting Bf109s with a fleeting burst, shot down Werner Andres - *Gruppen Kommandore* of II./JG27'. This does not fit my recollection as I was initially attacked by a Bf109. A more likely candidate for my claim was *Uffz* Heinz Uebe from 6./JG27, who was wounded but rescued. I then continued the pursuit of the Ju87s towards the Cherbourg Peninsula

but after a short burst ran out of ammunition. I then
returned to base at sea level. During the combat I saw five
parachutes descending towards the sea. During the
engagement both Sgt Hallowes and myself believed that we
were fired on by a Hurricane. There is no confirmation that
the *Luftwaffe* used a captured Hurricane in this
engagement.

The days battle over the convoy had cost four
merchantmen, sunk, six badly damaged by Stukas and three
ships sunk by German E-boats. In the air, the bulk of the
fighting was undertaken by 43 Squadron and 145 Squadron.
My Squadron claimed eight enemy aircraft destroyed and
seven probably destroyed. Our losses were two pilots killed,
Plt Off. Cruttenden and Plt Off. OeLofse. One of the
Squadron aircraft force landed and three damaged aircraft
returning to base. Of my own 'Blue' Section, Plt Off. Upton
force landed at Form Farm, Whitewell on the Isle of Wight.
Fortunately, he was uninjured. Sgt Hurry of 'Blue 2'
returned with his damaged aircraft to base.

On 12th August, 1940, six of us at cockpit readiness
were scrambled to 20,000ft. Sector Control reported a 500
plus bandits approaching from the southwest and vectored
us to intercept. We continued on the vector and, when I saw
specks ahead, I called 'Tally-Ho 300 plus at 12 o'clock'. The
specks soon grew into a large number of enemy bombers
and escorting fighters. The CO, Squadron Leader Badger,
agreed that my section should attack the fighters and
endeavour to keep them off his section while his section
attacked the bombers. However, as we joined for battle the
Bf109s were still well above us and, seemingly, staying
there. So I decided my section would initially attack the
bombers with the CO – after all, this was our primary task
and the enemy fighters could well come down when the
bombers were attacked. There was a formation of five
bombers below and ahead. I selected my target and told my
two young pilots to do the same and keep a sharp lookout
behind. As I broke away after my attack I saw them going
into attack. My target was diving away on fire and I saw two
others breaking formation and at least two were badly

damaged. On one, the undercarriage came partly down and on the other one engine was smoking. I told Blue 2 and 3 to rejoin me if he could see me and we would take on another bomber formation of five bombers.

While keeping a sharp lookout behind me I searched the sky for my 'sprog' pilot. I did not see him. I could see plenty of enemy fighters high above but none in the vicinity. I then positioned to attack another Heinkel bomber on the port side of a formation. I again told Blue 2 and 3 to join me if they could see me. Blue 2 acknowledged. I made a last attack on the bomber. I hit it again and saw it break formation. As I considered I must have been getting low in ammunition and so probably was my No. 2, I instructed him to return to base. I then dived away to sea level. In this sortie, I saw a large number of Bf109s high above but I did not see any come down to help the bombers.

On the 13th August 1940 the Squadron was scrambled and vectored to intercept a large formation of bombers expected to cross the coast in the vicinity of Rye at 20,000ft. We climbed steadily towards height, myself leading 'B' Flight some 2,000ft above 'A' Flight led by Sqn Ldr Badger. I gave the 'Tally-Ho bandits 3 o'clock'. I called the CO and said I was ideally placed for a head-on attack to break-up the bombers. The CO told me to carry on. I turned 'B' Flight head-on with the bombers, told my guys to select their targets and then continue to attack from the rear quarter. I opened fire out of normal range and continued as we closed into range at a closing speed of some 500-600 knots.

As I turned to attack from the rear I saw some of the bombers had split up. Two were diving away streaming smoke and flames. I selected a target in a formation of three for a rear quarter attack. I went in to close range, perhaps 100yds and saw I was hitting the He111. As I pulled away I was hit and the fuel in my gravity tank in front of the windscreen caught fire. As I recall I was about height 20,000ft. I side slipped port and starboard in an endeavour to extinguish the fire. I could not see through the windscreen because of flames. It started to get very hot in the cockpit and soon flames appeared. I had now lost considerable height side slipping in an endeavour to put out the fire. I realised that if I was going to bale out I could not leave it much longer.

I disconnected the oxygen and R/T, undid my safety harness, closed the throttle and opened the emergency hatch. I pointed the aircraft to open countryside and with my right hand on the ripcord I baled out. After clearing the aircraft I pulled the ripcord. There followed a welcome jerk. I was especially pleased as I had packed the parachute. After I had slowed, I took stock. I appeared to be at about altitude 3,000ft. The silence was almost deafening after the engine noise and clatter of guns being fired. Looking around I could see I was over familiar countryside somewhere between Haslemere and Midhurst. I could not see my aircraft or see or hear any other aircraft. As I neared the ground I could see I was going to land close to the edge of a wood. There was a slight wind and, as I landed, I drifted across some tree stumps, which did not do my ankle any good.

I had started to gather up my parachute. While doing this a voice from behind me said, in an authoritative tone 'Have you got any identification?' I turned and saw a stern looking constable. I replied 'No'. I explained who I was and which RAF base I came from and what had happened. It being an early morning sortie I only had pyjamas on under my flying suit. 'Dog tags' had not yet been issued.

The law then said I would have to accompany him to the local police station. I finished gathering up my parachute and followed the constable up a slight hill for about 100 metres to his car. There parked on the roadside in British racing car green colours was an MG two-seat sports car with the large rear tank – most un-police like vehicle in those days. In reply to my question the constable said it was a police vehicle. He opened the car door for me. I put my parachute behind my seat and got in the car. I asked where we were going, he replied 'Never you mind'. I realised he was being security conscious and viewed me with some suspicion. While being driven to the police station I explained in more detail to the constable what had happened. He made no comment.

After a few minutes drive we entered a small town and drew up at what was obviously the police station. I got out of the car, collected my parachute and was shepherded into the building. We pulled up at a desk behind which sat a formidable police sergeant. My escort explained how he had seen me descending in a parachute and how he had followed my descent and hastened to where I had landed. On questioning me he found I had no identification and brought me in. In reply to the police sergeant, I explained I was an RAF fighter pilot based at Tangmere. I gave my name and number and explained why I had no identification on me. I then asked the sergeant to telephone the Adjutant of 43 Squadron at Tangmere, explain the situation and ask him to send a car to collect me.

The sergeant continued to view me with suspicion. Without further ado he instructed a constable to lock me up in the cell with the others. He put me in a cell in which there were four other obvious aircrew dressed in flying kit. We looked at each other for a short time then one spoke to me in German of which I understood a little from schooldays. I asked in English who they were. One replied in English that they were what remained of the crew of two Heinkel bombers that had been shot down that morning. They were from an airfield in Northern France. I did not say that I might have been the one that had shot them down. It might have started something in the cell. In reply to their queries I explained I was an RAF pilot awaiting proof of identity. Conversation between us then became minimal and general.

After two hours or so the door of the lock-up opened and a constable came in, then escorted me out to the reception desk. There stood my friendly and unusually helpful Squadron Adjutant Stewart Carey. In reply to the police sergeant Stewart said he had never seen me before in his life. The sergeant ordered the constable to take me back to the cell. As the constable started to return me to the lock-up I began to protest vehemently, Stewart called stop and that he was only joking. The sergeant told me to sit down while he spoke with Stewart. The constable stood at my side. After another hour or so it seemed Stewart had convinced the police sergeant that he had only been joking and I was who I claimed to be. The constable was then sent to provide Stewart and I with a cup of tea. After a friendly chat with the two policemen we both prepared to leave. The police sergeant had a final word for both of us. To Stewart, 'Be careful to who and when you make jokes'. To me 'Carry your identification in future even when you are only wearing pyjamas'. We had a rather hilarious ride back to Tangmere.

The epilogue to this incident came some forty years later. In Australia, where I lived then, I received a parcel containing two pieces of metal from the engine of my aircraft. Later a piece of the shattered windscreen arrived. After I had pointed the aircraft into open country and baled out it had crashed on the farmland of Ian Hutton, not far from Liphook. We are now good friends and both supporters of the Hurricane Society. He had done a great deal of research to find me in Australia.

On 30th August, 1940, we lost our popular and capable CO, Sqn Ldr J V C Badger. 'A' flights two sections, 'Red' and 'Green', together with my 'Blue' Section, were ordered off from Tangmere at 1655 hours, to be followed by 'Yellow' Section eight minutes later, with orders to patrol Beachy Head at 20,000ft. 'Yellow' Section, unable to catch the rest of the Squadron, were ordered to patrol between Brighton and Beachy Head from where they failed to sight any enemy activity and returned to base. The remainder of the Squadron proceeded from Beachy Head in a northwest direction and eventually sighted formations of bombers with fighter escort over Ashford. The enemy formations consisted of an estimated fifteen to twenty Do 215s or Do 17s at a height of 21,000ft, and escorted by Bf109s. A series of individual 'dog fights' broke out and, in the mêlée of twisting and turning aircraft, 'Red 2' managed to get onto the tail of one Bf109 firing a short burst from astern at a range of about 250-200yds. While vapour started to appear from beneath the 109s fuselage, half rolling the enemy aircraft dived down closely followed by Red 2. Levelling out from its dive the white vapour appeared to have stopped but this was short lived when Red 2 delivered a second attack, again from astern at a range of 200 yards, causing a second puff of smoke or oil to pour from the retreating 109 and forcing it to go lower. 'Red 2' then broke away as he had exhausted his ammunition.

Meantime, Squadron Leader Badger, leading 'Green' section, had become involved in the general mêlée. Green 2 and 3 engaged individual bombers but we in 'Blue' Station did not see the results of their attacks. Only 'Blue 1', myself, of Blue Section was able to fire his guns, knocking pieces off a bomber. During the engagement Sqn Ldr Badger was shot down flying Hurricane V6548, which subsequently crashed south of Woodchurch. Sqn Ldr Badger, although grievously wounded, was able to jump clear. He landed by parachute in a tree and was admitted to Ashford Hospital with terrible internal injuries. Fighting his wounds for nearly a year Sqn Ldr Badger succumbed to his wounds and died on 30th June, 1941. He lies buried at Halton (St Michael and All Angels) Churchyard, Buckinghamshire, Plot 3, Row B, Grave 111. He had been one of us and in every respect he was a great loss.

On the 1st September, 1940, Flt Lt Caesar Hull was posted from 263 Squadron, promoted acting squadron leader, and assumed command of 43 Squadron. Earlier, as a junior officer, he served in No. 1 Squadron, the twin squadron of 43 Squadron at Tangmere in 1938. He was an experienced combat pilot having flown Gladiators in the Norwegian campaign and claimed a number of victories. He had an extrovert personality and was popular with the pilots and ground crews.

On 2nd September, 1940, I rejoined the Squadron after being shot down on 13 August, 1940, when I baled out. I have no recollection of being formally non-effective sick at this time and actually flew with the Squadron. This day was particularly sad for the Squadron as 'Wombat' Tony Woods-Scawen baled out for the seventh time. Unfortunately this time he did not survive. Plt Off. Carswell and Plt Off. Dan du Vivier were also shot down on this day. Both survived with injuries. On the credit side both Flt Lt Dick Reynell and Sgt Jeffries shot down Bf109s from 1./JG53.

On the 4th September, 1940, 43 Squadron, with two other squadrons, engaged a large formation of Me110s that were coming in over Worthing. It proved to be an attack on the Vickers and Hawker factories at Brooklands near Weybridge. It seemed that only Me110s carrying bombs were used in the attack. 43 Squadron engaged aircraft of Stab III./ZG76. One enemy aircraft was shot down by Plt Off. Upton on the Downs at High Salvington, near Findon. I engaged another aircraft in this raid and shot it down at Church Farm, Washington near Pulborough at 13.30pm. The aircraft dived straight into the ground with such force that no trace of the crew was found. Subsequently I ascertained the identities of the crew were *Oblt* H Florenz and *Gefr* R Herbert. (see Appendix 7)

After the above engagement I then joined a mixed bag of Hurricanes and Spitfires chasing another Me110. It was flying very low with a damaged port engine. In my attack I hit the aircraft and saw pieces coming off the tail. Further attacks forced the aircraft to belly land at Mill Hill near Shoreham Downs at approximately 1350 hrs. The pilot proved to be a *Geschwader* Adjutant *Oberleutnant* W Schaefer who was captured unhurt. His crewman, *Uffz* H Bendjus, was also captured but slightly injured.

On return to base I learnt the Squadron had had a successful day. In addition to the two Me110s claimed by myself, Plt Off. Upton, Plt Off. van der Hove and Sgt Jeffries each claimed a Me110. The Squadron had not suffered any losses. Unfortunately, the *Luftwaffe* targets at Brooklands had been severely damaged with large loss of life. It was estimated factory output would be severely affected for some two months. Fortunately the Hawkers Hurricane assembly shops had not been hit. An interesting postscript to this particular battle is that some 50 years later a fuel tank bracket take from the Me110 of Stab III./ZG76 that I shot down at Washington was presented to 43

Squadron as an 'Air Weapons Excellence Trophy' to be presented annually.

The 5th September, 1940, was a quieter day. When Sgt Hurry shot down a Bf109 of 5./JG27 at Eltham, Kent. The pilot of the Bf109 proved to be *Leutnant* Helmut Strobel who was killed. On the 6th September, 1940, at 0930 hrs, the Squadron was scrambled to patrol between Brooklands and Kingston at 10,000ft. While climbing to patrol the squadron was vectored to intercept a raid coming in over Dungeness. It turned out to be some fifteen to twenty bombers at 15,000ft supported by two groups of forty Bf109s at 20,000ft and 24,000ft, respectively. Weather was fine as usual that summer. My combat report below reflects the battle that 'B' Flight got into. It seemed the enemy effort was now changing from the convoys to the fighter airfields and radar chain.

I, as 'Blue 1' and leader of 'B' Flight, led my section to attack five Bf109s that were endeavouring to get on our tails. I attacked one Bf109 from behind and gave it one long burst. An explosion occurred in the port main plane and the aircraft commenced a steep dive towards the sea, issuing black smoke; I saw it and later three other aircraft crash into the sea nine miles off Dungeness. I presumed that two of these other three aircraft to be those shot down by Plt Off. Gorrie and Sgt Hurry. I climbed up again and attacked another Bf109 proceeding in a southerly direction. After one long burst I noticed damage to the wings and broke away as I saw it dive steeply. I did not see this aircraft again. As I climbed and turned to retain my attacking position I was hit by an aircraft that dived out of the sun. I too dived and turned steeply as my windscreen went opaque and I realised I had sustained an injury to my face. I pulled out and commenced a spiral climb to attack a Bf109. I aimed through the left hand side screen and hit the fuselage of the Bf109. I then dived again to ground level and proceeded back to base. Previously I had observed a further formation of Bf109s at 28,000ft and presumed that the aircraft that attacked me was one of these, who had chosen a favourable opportunity while I was climbing up. In view of the fact that

I was climbing and turning as tight as was compatible with climbing, the shooting of the enemy aircraft was excellent. All Bf109s that I observed had white noses and 'A' Flight dealt with the bombers.

Then there was noise in the cockpit as my gunsight and instrument panel disintegrated, and the windscreen shattered. I tightened my turn and peered through my side screens. I saw nothing. You never do see the one that gets you.

I did a couple of tight orbits. Saw nothing. Then I called up my No. 2, informed him I was low side combat and was returning to base. I dived to 5,000ft and as I levelled out I saw my wings being peppered again. I turned into the attack and saw a Bf109 go past. I straightened up, went after him and gave him a burst. I hit him. However, as I could only see him through my side screen and with no sight I assumed it would only be damage. I was pretty useless on the battlefield, so I dived down to tree level and headed for base.

Only then did I notice some blood on my flying suit and in the cockpit. I could not feel anything. I landed successfully and taxied in. Before I had stopped my ground crew, Bill Littlemore and Tommy Poole and one other who later I found out was my newest replacement Plt Off. Charles Palliser, of whom more later, had leapt on the wings and were unstrapping me and trying to lift me out of the cockpit. I found I could move normally as I got out of the cockpit. But there seemed to be a lot of blood about. The ambulance and station septic were on the spot before my feet touched the ground. I was taken straight off to station Sick Quarters.

Once there Doc cleaned me up and examined me. Apparently my face and neck had taken shrapnel from the Bf109 cannon shell that had exploded in the cockpit and glass from the gun sight, instrumentation panel and the shattered windscreen. My oxygen mask had saved some of my face. My goggles had been up and eyes exposed, cheeks, ears and neck also caught plenty. My good fairy had been with me and saved my eyes. She had probably saved my life.

The 7th September, 1940, was a Sunday. The day started quietly but near midday eleven aircraft of the squadron were scrambled. However, the raid the Squadron was scrambled for must have faded off the radar for soon after becoming airborne the Squadron was ordered back to base.

At about 1600 hrs on that same day a large build-up of enemy bombers and fighters was noted in the No. 11 Group and Sector Operations Rooms. The other two squadrons at Tangmere were scrambled and after being brought up to readiness state, nine aircraft of 43 Squadron were also scrambled at 1640 hrs. while other squadrons had been committed to meet the large raid, a second large build-up was observed in the Calais area. 43 Squadron was vectored to engage this force.   Most of the fighters had been committed to meet the initial large raid that appeared headed for London. Only 43 Squadron and a few other squadrons appeared available to deal with the second large raid. In the second raid, apparently, there were three groups of about twenty to twenty-five bombers and many more supporting fighters.

Caesar Hull, the CO who was leading the Squadron, told 'Killy' Kilmartin and his section to engage the fighters while the remaining six aircraft of the Squadron would deal with the bombers. After his initial command to attack the bombers, no more was heard from the CO. Flt Lieut Dick Reynell was also killed on this sortie. It seems he was fatally wounded, and baled out at a low altitude. Dick's aircraft crashed at Crown Point, Blackheath. Dick Reynell landed 100 yards away but he had died during his descent.

Dick Reynell was known to most of us pre-war pilots who had joined the RAF before the war. He became a test pilot and a good one at the Hawker Company who built the Hurricane fighter. He wanted to have a crack at the enemy. Caesar and I had tried to dissuade him, pointing out that he knew nothing of the tactics we had learnt in the air war. Caesar could have refused him outright, but Dick was very persuasive.

On the same sortie the Squadron also lost the CO, Caesar Hull. He was last seen diving to attack the bombers and may have been shot down by the escorting Bf109s. He was killed in his Hurricane that crashed in Purley High School grounds.

To complete this black day, Sgt Alan Deller was hit by cannon fire from one of the Bf109s but managed to bale out unhurt. He landed in an apple orchard at Babylon Farm, Sutton Valence, where a Spitfire had crash landed earlier.

On returning to Tangmere Killy Kilmartin took off his helmet and was heard to utter 'My God', that succinctly expressed his opinion of the debacle. At least Killy had shot down one of the Bf109s.

In the evening I was once again put on the strength of the Squadron officially. This was a paper transaction. I was also once again in temporary command of the Squadron after a CO had been shot down.

At this time our pilot strength in the Squadron was much weakened. Not only had we lost four Commanding Officers as the battle intensified, we had lost most of our combat trained pilots. A total of fourteen were killed in the Battle. Some were in hospital for the time being, some recovering from wounds. Some were several gallant replacements. John 'Killy' Kilmartin, the 'A' Flight Commander, myself, and six or seven replacements, were the only pilots available. Our maximum combat strength was really less than one flight.

A wise decision was taken by Fighter Command. Instead of filling us up with virtually new replacements that we could not train and maintain an operational state, we would be withdrawn to a less hectic area to rebuild and train up our replacements and still remain operational. 43 Squadron would be replaced by 607 Squadron, a unit that had not yet seen real front line battle action in the Battle.

On the 8th September, 1940, eleven Hurricanes of 43 Squadron took off from Tangmere and headed for Usworth, near Sunderland in the northeast of England, they were led by Flt Lieut. Kilmartin. The Squadron was replaced at Tangmere by 607 Squadron that had came from Usworth. The Squadron ground crew were flown up to Usworth in a transport aircraft but I remained at Tangmere for a few more days. During this time I helped 607 Squadron to settle in. Flt Lieut. Blackadder of 607 Squadron and I became friendly, and I flew with them. My logbook indicates that I flew on the 12th September, 1940, and continued each day until I left Tangmere for Usworth on the 19th September. On the 9th September, 607 Squadron had its introduction to the battle. On this day it lost six Hurricanes, three pilots killed, two wounded and one who baled out hurt. The Septic (doctor) also continued to remove bits of shrapnel and windscreen from my face and neck until I left Tangmere.

On the 16th September, 1940, I was promoted 'Acting' Squadron Leader and officially assumed command of 43 Squadron. I was honoured to be selected to command this famous 'Fighting Cocks' Squadron that had done well in World War One. I understand I held the command longer than any other squadron commander of any of the Fighter Command squadrons during the war. From its formation in 1916 near Stirling the Squadron was known for its *esprit de corps* and camaraderie among all ranks. I regarded that it was one of my priority tasks to maintain this spirit.

43 Squadron had made a major contribution to winning the Battle of Britain (see Appendix) and had suffered heavily. I am proud to have known and flown with these brave men.

CHAPTER SIX

13 Group

A T USWORTH we were required to continue operational readiness with four aircraft. Either Killy Kilmartin or I would use the other available aircraft for combat training of replacement pilots. Killy and I would also provide readiness at night to deal with intruders.

While the Squadron was at Usworth one of our earliest replacements was a Czech pilot called Joe Pipa. He was trained as a fighter pilot in the pre-war Czechoslovakian Air Force and fought against the Germans when they invaded his country. Escaping to Poland when Czechoslovakia was overrun, he escaped again when Poland was defeated and attempted to join the French Foreign Legion. However, he was seconded to the French *L'Armee de L'Air*, flying Potez fighters, where, in May 1940, he shared in the destruction of a Do17 and probable destruction of a Do215.

When France capitulated Joe escaped the Germans again. He found his way to Gibraltar and to England via ship around South Africa. He joined the Royal Air Force Volunteer Reserve (RAFVR) as an Aircraftsman 2nd Class (AC2) but was quickly promoted to Sergeant Pilot. After converting to Hurricanes at No. 6 Officer Training Unit (OTU) he was posted to No. 43 squadron, then at Usworth. We were glad to have such an experienced, skilful and gallant replacement. He was invaluable in helping us to train our young and inexperienced replacements. While he was with the Squadron he was recommended for a commission and awarded the Czech Military Cross. Later, after he had left us to join the Czech squadrons in the RAF Joe was awarded two bars to his Czech Gallantry Medal and the *Croix de Guerre* for his time with the *L'Armee de L'Air* and, in 1944, he was awarded the Czech War Memorial Medal. In 1946 when he was released from military service he was awarded the Czech Medal of Merit 1st Class. After gaining British citizenship he returned to the UK. He rejoined the RAF on a seven-year engagement and was promoted Flight Lieutenant in May 1956. He left the RAF in 1958. In June 1943 Joe married Marie Lilian Judge. He died of a heart attack on 2nd January, 1977, and was cremated in Swindon. He was an outstanding pilot and became my permanent No. 2. Whenever we flew over the airfield at Usworth and later Acklington, returning from a sortie, we would fly abreast and the wing of Joe's Hurricane would just touch my wing. I examined my wing tip one day and found a very small dent on the end of the wing where our wings had touched. It was the sort of thing we could do only when the air was very smooth with no bumps.

In December 1940 the Squadron was moved from Usworth, just south of the Tyne to Acklington North of the Tyne. After a short stay at Acklington the Squadron was moved north to Drem. This airfield was located near North Berwick and some ten miles east of Edinburgh. Immediately adjacent to the east of Drem was East Fortune airfield. This base was training crews on the Beaufighter night fighter that was just coming into service.

The Squadron was still required to provide four aircraft at readiness at Drem. Killy or myself would take the other available aircraft for combat training of replacement pilots. Killy and I would also provide readiness at night to deal with enemy aircraft intruders. From Drem, the Squadron could provide cover for the north, south, and over the Firth of Forth and also some limited cover at night, until the Beaufighter night fighter squadron at East Fortune became fully operational.

While at Drem I was to lose my Adjutant, the

indefatigable Stewart Carey who had served in World
War I as a fighter pilot. In this war he had been a loyal
and efficient Adjutant to my four predecessors and to
me. He was my very good friend and loyal supporter
and a great loss. After he was posted he was promoted
acting squadron leader and went to the personnel staff
at HQ Fighter Command, Bentley Priory, Stanmore,
where he continued to look after 43 Squadron.

First he arranged that our Intelligence Officer,
Geoffrey Marshall, another friend and stalwart, would
take over as Squadron Adjutant, a fitting replacement.
Then he found me another Flight Commander. There
had been a vacancy since I had become Squadron
Commander. Flt Lieut. Geoffrey May did not have
operational experience at the time, but he had
potential.

The main operational task by day was convoy
protection and interception of reconnaissance aircraft,
sometimes based on good tactical intelligence
information. This provided operational training for the
replacement pilots.

Combat readiness continued day and at night, even
though there was a Beaufighter night fighter squadron
working up at East Fortune airfield adjacent to us. Our
combat training of replacement pilots continued,
though most were sent to other squadrons when we
thought they were ready. For example, we had two
Polish officers, Grosewski, Malinowski and Sgt
Wilenski. A frequent visitor and a very pleasant and
competent night fighter pilot from 603 Squadron next
door was Ludwig Martel. All my Polish pilots went to
the Polish squadrons when ready, the Americans to the
Eagle squadrons and the French to the French
squadrons.

We had several successful interceptions by day and by
night at this time. My contribution was at night. This
was because only the most experienced pilots like Killy
and myself would be at readiness at night. The target at
night was mainly Glasgow, we would be on patrol and

be vectored on to a target, the targets would be seen either by being silhouetted against the fires they had lit or against cloud above or below them. On a moonlight night the moon would also be a help in locating a target and keeping it in sight. Once found, one would position astern and slightly below the target and use the red-hot exhausts to keep the target in sight and close in to firing range.

Stewart Carey, in his new personnel post at the Fighter Command sent his old squadron good quality replacements. We kept some to build up our pilot establishment again, others were sent south to Squadrons in the line, but as replacements with some combat training.

At Drem, the Squadron became notable for a few reasons. First, the pilots began to acquire an international flavour, apart from English, Welsh, Scottish and Irish pilots, Polish, Norwegian, French, American volunteers, Indian and West Indian and Belgian pilots began to arrive. At one time there were fourteen different nationalities in the Squadron at the same time. Most of these would leave us eventually to join their appropriate national squadrons that were being formed in Fighter Command.

The Belgians stayed with us. The senior one, Major le Roi du Vivier, gallant and popular with us all, succeeded me as Commanding Officer of the Squadron about a year later. Joe Mehta, a Hindu Indonesian, was a young and potentially good fighter pilot and popular with all the Squadron. Unfortunately, he was killed when he flew into a high hill north of Newcastle in bad weather. As his Commanding Officer I attended his funeral with some of his companion pilots in the Hindu temple in Newcastle. It was a very sad and moving occasion for us all.

On the 22nd January, 1941, Jim Hallowes, one of the Squadrons long serving stalwarts was posted from the Squadron. He was now commissioned and had a total score of seventeen enemy aircraft destroyed, two shared, four 'probables' and eight damaged. He had been awarded a Distinguished Flying Medal (DFM) and Bar before being commissioned and in June 1943 was awarded a Distinguished Flying Cross (DFC). He completed his service career as a Wing Commander.

Towards the end of January 1941, Drem and Turnhouse had to be temporarily closed because of heavy snow. 43 Squadron was moved across the Firth of Forth to the Royal Navy airfield at Crail – HMS *Jackdaw*. This was to enable the Squadron to remain operational. It returned to Drem on the 1st March, 1942.

On the night of 5/6 May, 1941, I was scrambled to intercept aircraft in a raid on Glasgow. I was vectored on to an aircraft that appeared to be leaving the target area. As I closed on the aircraft I recognised a Ju88. I closed range from below and behind and opened fire. I hit the Ju88 with several short bursts. It crashed into the sea off Anstruther. On my second sortie later that night I was vectored on to another probable Ju88. Again I attacked from below and behind and sent the aircraft crashing into the sea off Fifeness. In both cases, radar reported the plots faded at the time I reported the crashes. The crash in the sea of the second enemy aircraft was also reported to shore by a boat off Fifeness.

From examination of *Luftwaffe* records it would appear that the first claim above was a Ju88 A5(F) of II./KG54. The second claim was almost certainly another Ju88 A5(F) of 2.(F)122. The crew of both aircraft were all lost.

The following night, 6/7th, I intercepted and shot down another Ju88. I was flying a Hurricane II fitted with cannon and machine guns.

When on patrol Sector Control informed me that 'bandits' were approaching from the west at 8,000ft. I left the patrol line and flew south, climbing to about 9,000ft. I soon saw an enemy aircraft. I turned on to its tail and flight slightly below I closed to firing range. I fired a long burst. A flash occurred, the starboard engine appeared to pack-up and the starboard wing broke off. The Ju88 went into a spin and disappeared into cloud 10/10th at about 700ft. I was clear above.

The enemy aircraft Ju88 was from I./KG76 and all the crew were lost.

On the afternoon of 7th May our first day victory in 13 Group was claimed. Major le Roi du Vivier and Plt Off. Mize were on a training flight when they were vectored to intercept a Ju88. They shot it down into the sea.

This was the start of a good run for Roi du Vivier. On 10th May he again destroyed a Ju88, this time with Plt Off. Hutchinson. On 28th May he destroyed a third Ju88 that crashed at Boghall Hill, New Castleton.

After this run of victories in the day, night action returned on 8/9 June. According to my Combat Report, I took off from Drem at 2340 hours and headed for my patrol line at St Abbs Head at a height of 400ft. When on patrol some fifteen to twenty miles out to sea and at a height of 2,000ft I saw the shadow of an intruder on the moonlit sea a few miles east from a small vessel. I dived on the intruder and closed range to about 200 yards. I identified the aircraft as a Junkers 88. It was flying north-east at a height of about 1000ft, at about 200 knots. I opened fire with a short burst at a range of about 75 yards from dead astern and above. I fired a second short burst allowing less deflection. I hit the aircraft again. It then dived straight into the sea and broke up. I orbited the wreckage for approximately three minutes without seeing any sign of survivors. I returned to my patrol line at St Abbs Head until ordered to land.

Luftwaffe records revealed that the Ju88 was from 11./KG30 and that *Leutnant* Arno Hick and his crew were lost.

There was to be an interval of over a month before the Squadron and myself saw further action. On 11th July I took off at 0015 hrs with orders to investigate an

X raid east of Bell Rock. I saw two aircraft that appeared to be attacking a convoy when about twenty miles east of Bell Rock. When one of them was running up to attack a ship in the convoy, I gave chase and attacked the enemy aircraft twice from dead astern at close range. The enemy aircraft took no avoiding action nor gave any return fire. After my second attack the enemy aircraft crashed into the sea. Ships in the convoy subsequently confirmed that a He111 had been destroyed. The *Luftwaffe* reported a loss on this night of a Heinkel He111 H.5 off Hull with *Fw* L Weitz rescued and taken prisoner. The three other crew were missing.

In connection with this engagement the following telephone message was received via the Station Adjutant, Drem:

> 'AOC No. 13 Group AVM J O Andrews and Group Capt. The Duke of Hamilton, Turnhouse, offer their sincere congratulations to Sqn Ldr Morgan on his successful combat last night.'

Our night fighting force, initially Blenheims and later Beaufighters fitted with electronic air interception equipment, was being built up at this time late 1940-41. A night fighting role fell on the day fighters in the meantime, particularly in second and third phases of the moon. We day fighters could seek out the *Luftwaffe* bombers silhouetted against cloud or the fires they had lit. With good vectoring from Sector Control we could sometimes see the engine exhaust of the *Luftwaffe* bombers as we came up to attack from the rear.

When flying conditions were suitable for day fighters to find and destroy enemy bombers attacking targets in places such as Glasgow, Edinburgh and Rosyth Naval Base under the able control and direction of Turnhouse Sector Control, I was able to set out and destroy four enemy bombers, and damage some others. I had destroyed three when the Squadron was at Acklington.

We used to get tactical intelligence warning of some

of the daylight raids, particularly of the *Luftwaffe* reconnaissance flights. This enabled us to put up a patrol at the expected time and place. Sometimes, this resulted in a successful interception. On 24th July, as a result of information, I put up two sections, two aircraft on different patrol lines, about 20 miles out to sea, between the Firth of Forth and St Abbot's Head. I took up a new boy for training. We patrolled behind the other two sections as back-up and closer to the coast. My No. 2 was Pilot Officer Bourne who was eventually invalided out of the RAF.

I was flying south with Bourne on our patrol line when we spotted an aircraft flying in from the east and about to cross the English coastline. This looked like the recce. Bourne and I opened our throttles and the extra boost facility and started to climb. As soon as he saw us the enemy aircraft turned east. It was a Ju88 at about 3-5,000ft altitude. We turned to follow. We were now well above it. I told my No. 2 to prepare to attack and follow me in. The Ju88 seemed to be flying at about 2,000ft. We commenced a steep diving attack from the rear quarter. We were closing fast into firing range from above when my engine stopped. While I was out of firing range my excess speed in the dive allowed me to continue close to firing range. I opened fire and hit the Ju88 and its undercarriage came down. I continued firing until I was at 150 yds range then broke away.

I then called Bourne and told him to go in and finish off the Ju88. I then informed him I was going to ditch and after he had finished off the Ju88 to climb up and give our approximate position to Sector Control. I then prepared to ditch. I noted the direction of waves so that I would land parallel. I disconnected my radio and oxygen and foolishly unclicked my safety strap. Then I opened the emergency escape panel and finally checked my dinghy harness. Now I concentrated on my approach and wheels up landing in the water. As I flattened out for the landing I held the nose higher than usual so that the large air intake under the centre of the aircraft would hit the water as the aircraft stalled on to the water and not drag my aircraft under water. I put my left hand over the gun sight to protect my face as the aircraft hit the water.

The Hurricane did stall on to the water with little forward motion and remained afloat for sufficient time for me to get out of the cockpit, walk along the wing and detach my parachute from the dinghy. I then unscrewed the cap of the compressed air or CO_2 bottle to inflate the dinghy. Nothing, the bottle was empty. I resorted to the hand pump. It was made of Bakelite and had broken into small pieces, presumably where I had been sitting on it. I managed to hold the pieces together and partially inflate the dinghy, then the aircraft started to sink. I inflated my 'Mae West' life jacket and climbed into the dinghy, my feet were out of the water, and so was my upper body. I continued to pump for a while but to little or no avail.

My No. 2 was still orbiting overhead. After a while he was relieved by a section of two from the Squadron. I then noticed that the section was being led by my own No. 2, Joe Pipa. A sure sign that all would be well. Joe then flew low over and me and threw out another life jacket that I collected and tied to my own. Joe then flew over me again, low and slow and pointed in an Easterly direction. I did not see anything at first but when I went to the top of the next wave in the swell I saw two men in a round dinghy. I indicated to Joe that I had seen them. Obviously, they could only be the crew or some of the crew from the Ju88 that Bourne and I had downed. The last squadron section flew over me and departed as dusk fell. I was getting colder and I could feel there was something wrong with my mouth. I was already regretting that I had left undoing my safety straps till after the aircraft had ditched.

The night of course grew colder, as did I. There were some rain showers and the wind increased. Occasionally the moon peeped from between the clouds. At last, dawn broke. The showers had ceased and it looked as

Drem 1941, *left to right*, TDM. Ray Harries. I.O., two American pilots.
Front left to right, Sgt Mills, Sgt Pipa. *(via Bill Littlemore)*

Drem 1941, TDM in an aerial shot taken by 'Bush' Cotton.
(via Andy Thomas)

Drem 1941. Ray Harries with his ground crew, F/Sgt Savage, George Boyd and Bert Morley. *(via Bill Littlemore)*

Drem 1941. My excellent wing man, Joe Pipa, *(via Bill Littlemore)*

RAF Staff College 17th War Course, April 1946. TDM is standing in the centre of the picture *(top row)*. *(Gale & Polden)*

Queen Mary's visit to 10 Group HQ. TDM is standing immediately behind the Queen with Air Vice-Marshal Steele on her left.

TDM helped escort a number of American formations and almost all their..

.....planes carried individual insignia ......here are a few examples.

TDM's Vampire during his time at Gutersloh.

TDM *(left)* taking tea with Sir Hector McGregor, AOC 2 Group, Germany, during a display by the Gutersloh Vampire Wing in 1950.

The Gutersloh Vampires during the display for 'Top Brass' in 1950.

TDM's brother,
John.

TDM as Group Captain in
Germany, 1951.

though it could be another fine day. My watch had stopped but of course I knew it must be between four and five o'clock am. An hour or so later the first section from the Squadron found me, the section orbited me enabling Sector Control to calculate my position.

By the time the Fourth Section, Joe leading again, arrived over the top it must have been around midday or a little later by the sun position. I ate a couple of Horlicks tablets from my emergency rations but I was more thirsty. Joe then flew low and slow over me to draw my attention. I looked towards the east first thinking Joe was drawing my attention to the German airmen in their raft. However, he made another run over and I realised he was pointing west. I looked in that direction and saw smoke on the horizon. One of the Section flew between the ship and my position. As the smoke on the horizon grew in to a four funnel destroyer and approached me I realised I would soon be rescued. I later found out that the destroyer was HMS *Ludlow*, one of fifty such ships the USA had traded with the UK for the use of Goose Bay airfield in Newfoundland.

The destroyer stopped some hundreds of yards from me and put a rafter dinghy over the side that motored towards me. Soon it was alongside me and two of the three sailors helped me aboard and at my request picked up my dinghy. On return to the destroyer I was hoisted aboard and was met by the Commander who was the Captain and two or three officers, one of whom was the doctor.

I was taken below and offered a tot of rum. I thanked my host as best as I could, for my mouth felt a mess, and said I would prefer a coffee. This soon arrived with a straw to drink it. The Commander then told me he would rejoin the convoy he was escorting and I would be put ashore as soon as arrangements could be made. I expressed my very sincere thanks for rescuing me, then the doctor escorted me to the sick bay. Here I was cleaned up, provided with warm dry clothes, medically examined and then put in a warm bed. The doctor then explained my jaw was fractured and my upper and lower front teeth were loose in my mouth but still attached to some of the gum. If there was much delay in getting me ashore he would have to operate. He gave me a sedative and told me to relax and try to sleep. This I must have done but when I awakened the Commander came alongside and told me the RAF Air Sea Rescue launch from Felixstowe had run late and missed us as we sailed north with the convoy.

Two further attempts were made to take me off. One from Hull and the other from Rosyth in the Firth of Forth. Both were late and failed to intercept us. The Commander came down to see how I was and told me that if the next attempt to take me off at Aberdeen failed, I would go to the USA with them. The Doctor said he would have to operate. I realised that would put me out of the war for quite a while and I would lose my Squadron. This was, to say the least, upsetting. I dozed off for a while thinking how was I going to get back into the fighting and how soon.

I was woken by the Doctor and the Commander's No. 2, standing at his side. He told me that they had fortunately intercepted the Aberdeen herring fishing fleet returning to port and that I was going to be transhipped to one of the fishing boats and be taken ashore. This was good news. Without more ado I was taken on deck and strapped into a hammock. After saying my adieus and thanks to the Commander, Doctor and crew standing around, I was lowered over the side into the rubber dinghy and motored over to a waiting fishing boat where I was lifted on to the deck by Navy personnel and fishermen. The fishing boat Skipper then told me I would have to remain on deck as they could not get me below in the hammock. The Doctor had told him I was to be left in the hammock. We would be met on the wharf by an ambulance that would take me to the Naval Hospital at Kingsent. We should be in port in a couple of hours.

The convoy had left us an hour or so, or so it seemed, when I heard aircraft with what was clearly not a British engine sound. I warned the Skipper to keep a sharp lookout. Next I heard cannon fire and a couple of explosions. The Skipper said some of the fishing boats were being straffed and bombed but the bombs were missing. I could not see anything strapped in the hammock but heard the Skipper call, 'Lookout, our turn next'. The crew quickly went below before the straffing commenced. Fortunately for us, it was mostly inaccurate. The Skipper was slightly wounded in one arm and there were a few holes in the deck. As the aircraft passed over I could see it was a Ju88. There were no further attacks and soon the crew re-appeared and came over to see how I was. One went to the bridge to see how the Skipper was. I heard him say he was alright except for a slight scratch. The fishing fleet continued on its way to port without further incident.

As we arrived in harbour the other boats allowed ours to proceed ahead and berth right alongside the wharf where the ambulance awaited our arrival. After we had tied up, the Skipper and crew lifted me ashore where I taken over the by ambulance crew. I gave my thanks and appreciation to the Skipper and crew for accepting me from the destroyer and bringing me ashore.

The ambulance then set off for Kingsent Naval Hospital to the south of Aberdeen. On arrival, I was admitted to the examination room to be seen by the doctor and the dental surgeon. The doctor expressed satisfaction with the progress of my fractured jaw. The dental surgeon said that I must go into the operating theatre immediately for him to start work on my mouth and teeth. I was wheeled into the operating theatre and given an anaesthetic. Next, I woke up in the recovery room with a nurse carefully wiping away a little blood around my mouth. The dental surgeon came in later and asked how I felt, he said the operation had been a complete success. All my front teeth, upper and lower,

had been wired back into position. He expected me to
be in hospital under his care for two-three weeks then
become an outpatient.

While in hospital I was visited by Mr and Mrs
Hutchinson, the parents of one of my replacement
pilots. After speaking with the dental surgeon they
insisted that I should stay with them when I became an
outpatient. I made good progress and was discharged
from hospital on 1st August, 1941, and granted twenty-
eight days leave. I then spent a very pleasant time with
Mr and Mrs Hutchinson. The dental surgeon then said I
could return to Drem, but I was to report to the dentist
at Turnhouse, our Sector, Headquarters, near Edinburgh
every four to five days. He would be briefing the dentist
at Turnhouse. I also agreed that provided it did not
interfere with my operational flying I would attend one
or two dental symposiums with him so that he could
show off his work. I then departed Aberdeen by train
for Edinburgh. Here, I was met enthusiastically by my
pilots and flight sergeants Parker and Yates of 'A' and 'B'
flights, respectively, and driven back to Drem. The next
day I was flying.

The *Luftwaffe* aircraft that we engaged was a Ju88D-
2 of I(F)120 that had crashed into the sea off Hay Is,
Firth of Forth. All the crew were reported missing,
believed killed. As I have said I saw two of the crew in
a round dinghy some 1500 yds from where I was
rescued. Plt Off. Bourne said he saw crew in the water
but not in the dinghy. This may well have been the other
two members of the Ju88 crew. I reported to the
Commander of HMS *Ludlow* that I had seen two of the
Ju88 crew in a dinghy. He indicated that he could not
spend more valuable time away from the convoy
searching for them.

The dinghy I had used was a prototype for field tests.
After the ditching in the North Sea I went to
Farnborough and to RFD and told them of my
experience with the dinghy. I recommended more
checks on the CO_2 bottle before packing to ensure it

was full and did not leak; and the hand pump he re-located in a position in the dinghy pack where it would not be damaged when the pilot sits on the parachute and dinghy.

My final victory at Drem was on the night of 2nd October, 1941. I took off from Drem at 2140 hrs to patrol Berwick-on-Tweed at 14,000ft. While on patrol 20 miles off the coast I sighted an intruding enemy aircraft. It was flying 2,000ft lower than me. I dived below the enemy aircraft and positioned myself below and astern, closing to 400 yards where I identified the aircraft as a Ju88 in black camouflage. I closed to 200 yds and opened fire. There was intense return fire until I fired a second burst at 150 yds closing to 100 yds. The third burst raked the fuselage of the fleeing aircraft and set it alight. The Ju88 went into a steep dive, became engulfed in flame and crashed into the sea. The loss of this Ju88 cannot be traced in *Luftwaffe* records. Its crash into the sea was confirmed by the conjunction of the pilot's report of the crash and the fading of the radar dot.

The Squadron was relocated at RAF Acklington near Newcastle-upon-Tyne on 4th October, 1941. While at Acklington the Squadron participated in the field experiments for the development of the Havoc Turbinlite and day fighter system for night fighting. The Turbinlite was a powerful light installed in the nose of converted Havoc fighters. The Havoc also had electronic air-interception equipment. The Havoc and fighter would take-off together and seek out the enemy using sector control and the Havoc A1. When the Havoc and fighter were almost within firing range the Havoc would illuminate the enemy aircraft. The fighter would then move in and attack the illuminated enemy aircraft. The flying development was carried out by 43 Squadron at Acklington, and also another squadron in the West of England. After some flying experiments the system was abandoned. The Beaufighter night fighter equipped with A1 and guns was clearly going to be a more flexible system that eventually would take over the night fighter role completely from the day fighters.

When I was at Drem I was given the task, in conjunction with Major John Profumo, of developing a communication system between air fighters and advancing front line troops who were being held up by such German defences, such as tanks, pill boxes and other machine gun posts in farmhouses. Jack Profumo, as was known, became War Minister after the war.

He and his signals unit and I with my aircraft and ground crew were sent to a small airfield near Glasgow to develop the communication system. For us, the RAF, it just seemed a matter of allocating one of our eight VHF channels as required for the task. For the Army, it seemed it would be necessary to develop a lightweight VHF/FT transmitter/receiver that could readily be carried by or with advancing troops. Within three or four weeks we had an air/ground R/T system that could be suitable for the task. The Army would have to decide whether or not it could be carried by the forward troops or by a signals unit supporting them. As I recall, the Army decided on the latter. This did not burden the forward troops with more equipment. They would call for air assistance on their normal net and the signals unit would then call down the aircraft allocated from a cab rank of aircraft assigned for such close support tasks.

I found Jack Profumo easy and co-operative to work with on this task. Most of the work was on the Army side. On our side, it was allocating a VHF/RT frequency and proving the system in several flight tests, the reliability of the air/ground communication system. Jack would disappear at weekends and reappear ready for work on the Mondays with luxuries for both his and my troops. We lost a good man in our Government when Jack was forced to retire from his position as War Minister.

When I returned to Drem the work of rebuilding the strength of the Squadron, maintaining an operational state and providing some replacement pilots to squadrons in the south, continued unabated. Then in March 1942, after commanding a squadron for the longest period during wartime in Fighter Command, I was posted to HQ 13 Group, Fighter Command near Newcastle-upon-Tyne. I recommended that Flt Lieut. Le Roi du Vivier succeed me as Squadron Commander. Dan, as he was known, had shown himself to be an outstanding leader, popular with all ranks in the Squadron. With the support of Sqn Ldr Stewart Carey, in Personnel at Fighter Command, Dan became Commanding Officer No. 43 Squadron. He took Joe Pipa, my flying No. 2, as his No. 2 and I knew he would be well looked after.

Editor's note;   The effect that Tom had on 43 Squadron cannot be overstated. The following is an extract from the History of 43 Squadron *by Jim Beedle (Beaumont Aviation Literature, 1966):*

The two 'longest ever' records were set up at this time. 5th December 1940 to October 1941 was the longest stay on any one airfield during the war, while Sqn Ldr TFD Morgan (September 1940 – January 1942) recorded the longest spell of any a Commanding Officer. To him, more than any other, goes the credit for the performance of 43 during those days. Meeting all the operational commitments from Group and at the same time to achieve the maximum output of trained pilots necessitated a great deal of hard slogging and intensive application, the end products of which departed then to squadrons in the south! This was done, moreover, at a time when the training establishments were beginning to release a flood of both aircrew and tradesmen resulting in a high throughput and constant change of personnel. The old, long-fostered Squadron spirit could easily have been lost in this welter of a shifting manpower whose conditions of service were not conducive to the generation of regard or affection for the Squadron. For these birds of passage were, if aircrews, mostly anxious to be off to more active theatres of war, and the ground crews were still in the main bewildered and slightly resentful civilians whose self esteem had been crushed in the recruit-training centres and subsequently powdered in the processing through the soul-less cramming systems of wartime technical training. They had not yet had time to re-orientate themselves into a realisation that they were essential parts in the overall scheme and had yet to experience the boost to morale and self respect that such awakening to the fact that they were essential brought in its train. Yet, in spite of all these unfavourable factors, in spite of the fact that there was little in the basic routine of Squadron duties to stimulate morale, it remained high and showed no traces of decline. There was always a nucleus of technicians sufficiently permeated by the old traditional way of doing things better than most to ensure that the ancient customary habits did not fade away, and Morgan had a marked perspicacity for selecting the best out of the considerable number of pilots who came and went quickly during this time, and these chosen few tarried a while, acted as instructors and flew on ops. They were the successors to the survivors from Tangmere who during the last months of 1940 drifted away to command squadrons or pass on their knowledge as OTUs.

Nor only as a chief conservator of 43's tradition must Morgan be remembered, for his other deeds were of an order that few could hope to equal. If the leadership that command implies is best to be achieved by example, then Morgan was a remarkably successful commander and outstanding in the matter of demonstrating the technique of destruction by single engine fighters of enemy night bombers.

Inherent in its design the Hurricane, as a night-fighter, compared to its own disadvantage with the

specialised Beaufighter or the more adaptable
Defiant and Blenheim. Only in the Hurricane did the
pilot have the dual task of flying and searching. For
him there was no airborne radar, no radar operator
to provide the solace of human company and to
watch for the blip on the screen that located the
distant unseen quarry. There was nothing but the
lonely darkness, a darkness in which the enemy lay
hidden and for whom the search was made even
more difficult by the distortion of vision through the
propeller blades and the restriction of the exhaust
stub anti-dazzle plates forward of the cockpit;
moreover, condensation on hood or windscreen was
never completely eliminated by anti-mist pastes and
powders. Small wonder that under such conditions
very few night bombers ever fell victim to single-
seater fighter pilots and all the greater glory that
Tom Morgan, hunting quite alone, should have
destroyed no fewer than six in just under as many
months. Each one was a triumph of determination,
extraordinary night vision and the essential ability,
once in contact, to shoot straight first time before
the quarry, alerted by the opening burst of gunfire,
slipped as so easily it might, into the sheltering
blackness of the night.

Before I left the Squadron I had a phone call from a
very old friend, Flt Lt Harry Tennant. We had trained
together and been in 22 Squadron together. He was
subsequently posted to 36 Squadron, Singapore. He was
now home. Was there a chance that he could be posted
to 43 Squadron? Stewart Carey and I tried hard to get
him, as he was a good officer and a good pilot, just what
are needed as a Flight Commander in the Squadron and
a potential Squadron Commander. Unfortunately,
despite Stewart's and my efforts we could not get him,
apparently when an officer is posted home from
overseas his future is in the hands of Air Ministry
postings. In Harry Tennant's case he was posted in to
Fighter Command, but to one of the Polish Squadrons as

Flight Commander. Not long after, while leading a formation, a Polish pilot ran into him. Both the Pole and Harry were killed – a great waste.

CHAPTER SEVEN

HQ 13 Group

IN MARCH 1942 I was posted from the Squadron, still at Drem, to a staff job at HQ13 Group. I was promoted to the rank of Acting Wing Commander in the post of Operations. My task was to co-ordinate the disposition of operations and training of the 13 Group squadrons. To assist in the task there was an Operations Room manned, on a 24 hours basis, by three squadron leaders and their assistants, and the plotting table was operated by women from the Women's Auxiliary Air Force (WAAF). There were also liaison officers with the Observer Corps, AA guns and the Royal Navy.

An interesting job, but my main aim from the day I arrived at the Headquarters was to get back to operational flying. I knew this would take some time so I got stuck into the interesting staff job I had been given. It included visits to the sectors and the squadrons to check on the performance of the latter and squadron commanders and to hear their complaints and, if justified, endeavour to do something about them. Occasionally, to keep my hand in, I obtained a flight in one of the squadron Hurricanes or Spitfires. Eventually I wangled my own Spitfire at Group HQ.

On 27 March, 1942, the Air Officer Commanding (AOC) called me in to his office and said he wanted me to fly him to a little known near airfield, Tealing, North of Montrose, the next day. I was to check the destination airfield and weather forecast. We would fly via Turnhouse to pick up the Sector Commander, Group Capt. Guinness.

Next day, a dry forecast to be fine for flying, we took off for Turnhouse near Edinburgh at 0600 hours. On landing we were met by Group Capt. Loel Guinness and taken to the

Mess for coffee.

After a short stay we returned to our aircraft. Before we climbed aboard Loel said he noted that I was cold. So he had brought a service greatcoat for me. I said I would be glad to borrow it. He said I could keep it as he helped me into it. As he did so, I saw that it was lined with fur of what had been an expensive ladies coat. As I remonstrated he repeated I was to keep the coat, which I did and used until I left the Service in 1951.

We then took off and headed North for Tealing, not far from Montrose. On arrival over the airfield it proved to be one runway with unprepared surrounds and a single taxi-way to one Nissen hut. I landed carefully! To get off the runway would have been disastrous. I taxied to near the hut where I stopped. We disembarked and went into the hut. It was laid out for a reception, we were given coffee and sandwiches. The AOC then told Loel and myself that we had come to meet some Russian politicians who were flying in a Russian bomber. The Government representatives present told us that the main reception party from London, both British and Russian, had been killed in the aircraft flying them up to Tealing when it caught fire and crashed. We then heard a drone overhead and went outside to see the Russian bomber orbiting the strip. The pilot landed carefully and taxied slowly to the only small aircraft parking area near the hut. When the four engines were stopped, a door in the fuselage was opened, a ladder let down and six fully armed Red Army soldiers stepped out first, surrounded the aircraft with arms at the ready, then out came the official party of about twelve. The AOC, Loel and some of the British diplomats then went forward to greet the visitors but waited for them outside the circle of guards around the aircraft. They then took the Russians into the hut for refreshments.

I talked to the airmen through an interpreter and they had apparently flown on a northerly track to avoid flying over Germany. The weather had been variable and rough over Scandinavia and the North Sea. They had been briefed and given maps by the British air attaché in Moscow and given landmarks to help them find the airfield. Montrose had also been briefed to intercept the Russian bomber and sent it into the destination airfield. RAF Montrose had also been briefed to re-fuel the Russian aircraft for the return flight.

A very convivial party developed between the Russians and the British diplomats. It seemed the Russians had brought vodka with them. The Russian aircrew were looked after by we British airmen and the Russian aircraft guards were eventually brought in for something to eat. Two coaches then arrived to convey the diplomats to Dundee. Transport also came from Montrose with a re-fuelling party and to convey the aircrew and guards back to Montrose where they would stay until the return flight via Turnhouse to drop off Group Capt. Guinness and refuel.

Later, we heard that the Russian party would all now go by train as a result of the crash. The aircraft that crashed bringing the British and Russian reception party from London apparently affected the consultations between the Russians and the British for a while, as the former thought the aircraft accident was sabotage.

For the remainder of my stay at HQ13 Group work I returned to the normal staff duties required. I also continued my vigorous but diplomatic efforts to get back to operational flying. In late 1942, with the help of good friends on my behalf, I succeeded.

CHAPTER EIGHT

Ibsley Wing

O N THE 11th September, 1942, I was posted to Tangmere as Supervising Wing Commander, Flying, where over the next few weeks I flew several missions with the Wing that included fighter sweeps and bomber escorts. I understood that eventually I might take over the Wing. However, this was not to be and I was shortly posted to Middle Wallop, where I was to form a new Wing.

I reported to Group Capt. J Hardy who was the Senior Commander at Middle Wallop. After much friendly discussion and consultation by both of us with the AOC/Group it was agreed that I could live at Ibsley and assemble the three, and later four, Spitfire squadrons there. The Wing would also include the two Whirlwind squadrons at Warmwell and, later, a Canadian Mustang squadron that would be based at Middle Wallop. This made what became known as the Ibsley Wing, the biggest in Fighter Command. The station commander at Ibsley was Arthur Donaldson, who I knew. He was one of the intrepid Donaldson brothers.

My first objective was to get the Spitfire squadrons thinking and flying as a wing. We did a few fighter sweeps to enable the Spitfire squadrons to operate in the different tactical positions, e.g., lead squadron, middle cover squadron flying above and down sun of the lead squadron, top cover squadron flying above the other two. Also, take off and landing sequences or drifts and briefing and de-briefing. Lastly, rendezvousing with our Whirlwind squadrons to ensure they did not waste their fuel and later with our own Mustang squadron. We became a close knit

wing. For our own shows such as shipping recces the
Spitfires and the Mustangs would rendezvous with the
Whirlwinds over the Whirlwind base at Warmwell.
Rendezvous with bombers for fighter escorts and support
would be arranged through 10 Group HQ with the
bombers. The Whirlwinds would not participate in bomber
support operations because of their short range.

For our own shows, such as shipping reconnaissance, the
Mustangs would lead as anti-flak, the Whirlwinds would
carry two 500lb bombs each and the Spitfires would provide
escort and support. Either we would receive intelligence
information on enemy shipping in the Channel, or, we
would have sent out a recce sortie or two to locate shipping
for an attack. Sometimes we would escort our Whirlwinds
and Mustangs against railway, airfield and bridge targets.
This was good operational training.

In 1942 the RAF was on the offensive and carrying the
fight to the enemy. However, the *Luftwaffe* would hardly
react to our fighter sweeps. We needed the bombers to hurt
him and force the fighters to react. 2 Group RAF was now
equipped with Boston bombers and the USAF force of
Marauders, Fortresses and fighters in the UK was growing
steadily. So, increasingly our task was bomber support. Our
Spitfires range usually enabled us to support the Bostons on
penetration, over the target and withdrawal. We could only
support the Fortresses as far as fuel would allow our
maximum radius of action. The *Luftwaffe* fighters would
then standoff beyond our radius of action and wait to attack
the Fortresses after we were forced to return to base. We
could see the enemy fighters waiting for us to turn and then
go into attack the bombers.

More often than not, we moved to advance bases
temporarily to the East or to the West to improve our radius
of action in support of the bombers. For our Spitfires we
also had 30-gallon, 60-gallon and 90-gallon auxiliary
external drop tanks to extend our radius of action. These of
course would have to be dropped as soon as combat
appeared imminent. The fuel in these tanks was of course
used first from take-off. The tanks affected combat

manoeuvrability adversely.

The factory where the tanks were made was not far from Ibsley. I visited it one day to explain and emphasise how valuable a contribution their work made to our operations. The tanks were mainly made and tested by women. After my talk to them, two of the ladies stepped forward and gave me a Rosary and the other gave me a St Christopher on a chain. Not being of the faith, I put the Rosary safely into a drawer. I wore the St Christopher on the chain for some long time. It then caused a rash and irritation on my chest, so I also put it in the drawer.

Sometime later in 1943 the Wing was moved west, as we often were, to Harrowbeer, not far from Exeter. We were equipped with long-range tanks. I thought it would be another bomber support operation. After forty-eight hours sitting on the deck awaiting orders, I rang Group HQ and asked what was the situation. I was told to standby and continue to await further orders. I replied that if we were to continue at Harrowbeer another day we would need to send for some of our ground crews to maintain maximum serviceability. Early on the third day we were told the operation had been cancelled and we were to return to our base at Ibsley.

Much later I thought I had found out why it was cancelled. A US Army Assault Force was doing a top secret final rehearsal on the beaches at Slapton, South Devon. The Germans must have got word of the operation. The Assault Force got well out to sea and as they were turning back for the practice assault, they were attacked by a German Naval Force and were badly mauled with severe casualties. 946 US sevicemen died with ten missing officers who knew about D-Day, which could have compromised the invasion had they been captured. As a result, the invasion was called off until their bodies had been recovered. However, I also discovered that this took place in April 1944 and could not have been the cause of our cancelled operation, which took place a year later.

On another occasion the Wing was moved east to support 2 Group Bostons attacking targets in the Kiel area. On arrival at our advance base at Coltishall I was informed that there would need to be a VHF practice frequency change in our aircraft for the operation. This was necessary from time to time on bomber support operations. As take-off time drew near, only a few of the aircraft were ready. An unusually long time was being taken to change to the frequencies if it really was necessary.

At take-off time I led a few aircraft (five or six) in which the frequency had been changed to meet with the bombers at the rendezvous place and time. On arrival at the rendezvous we saw the bombers approaching. Some eighteen to twenty Bostons. As we turned on to the outward course I realised we fighters were too few to adequately support the bombers in what would be a heavily defended area. I called up the bomber leader and told him I was aborting the operation because he had insufficient fighter support. I also went ahead of the bomber leader and waggled my wings as a confirmatory washout signal. On return to Coltishall I was told the AOC 12 Group wished to speak to me. In reply to his questions I told him I had to abort the operation because the majority of my aircraft had been grounded at take-off time with radio sets removed from the aircraft undergoing frequency change. With the few fighters that had become airborne I could not give the bombers adequate protection so I aborted the operation. I also told him that I had looked into the situation and that the frequency change had been unnecessary. I then spoke to my AOC 10 Group and explained what happened so that he heard the correct story. He agreed with my action.

There was another occasion when I thought it was necessary to abort the operation. It was in the early days of USAF bomber support. The target was Abbeville Railway Manufacturing Yards. A target which meant a very shallow penetration over the French coast and which would enable us to provide support all-round, penetration, target and withdrawal support. My wing was close escort. The other two wings were providing cover. As we left the rendezvous, I recall probably Beachhead, it seemed to me we were flying North of track for Abbeville. As we crossed the French coast this proved correct. Soon afterwards Abbeville could be seen some twenty to thirty miles in the distance at 3 o'clock. I expected the bombers to alter course to starboard and head for the target. Instead they continued heading east.

After a few minutes I noticed the two covering wings turn for home. They had no long range tanks so were at their maximum radius of action. I realised the time would soon come for my wing to turn for home. As the bombers were now well past their designated target I decided to abort the mission. At that time we had no fighter/bomber radio link, so I flew in front of the bomber leader and waggled my wings, the standard washout signal. I then flew alongside him to make sure he understood. He did, and we were soon heading home. There was an attempt to attack the bombers on the way, but we successfully fended them off without loss, with one or two victories over Bf109s. On landing back at our base at Hawkinge to re-fuel and re-arm as necessary. I reported to our Group HQ. Then I spoke with our liaison officer, Wing Cdr Walker at HQ USAF, High Wycombe and explained what had happened. I said that I thought that there could have been a navigation error right from the rendezvous point. Johnny rang me back later and told me that this was correct. The training of USAF navigators was not quite keeping up with expansion of the bomber force. However, this situation steadily improved. The USAF navigators growing familiarity with the European topography also assisted.

As the RAF and USAF bomber assault grew on strategic targets in Germany and in German held territories on the European continent, our fighter support of the bombers task predominated. Some fighters were still held at readiness in case of an attack by the *Luftwaffe*. However, when the *Luftwaffe* air assault on the UK failed in the autumn of 1940, Hitler cancelled Operation *Sea Lion*, the invasion of the UK and opened up a second front against Russia with whom he had a non-aggression pact. He left sufficient naval, ground air resources in the West to hold his conquests. The bulk of his forces were diverted to the East for his assault on Russia.

Meanwhile, the Royal Navy and Coastal Command were fighting the hard Battle of the Atlantic. After the defeat of France, the German Navy had quickly established two submarine bases – one at Lorient and one at St Nazaire on the west coast of France in the Bay of Biscay. In 1943 part of Coastal Commands operations was to invest these two ports with North-South patrols across the Bay of Biscay. This was an endeavour to catch the U-boats on the surface as they left the ports to patrol the North Atlantic for convoy targets and to catch them on the surface as they returned from patrol.

Coastal Command used Sunderland flying boats and Liberators aircraft for this task. As the Germans became aware of these patrols the *Luftwaffe* used their Fw190 fighters from the airfield at Brest-Guipavaz to find and destroy the Sunderlands and Liberators.

Coastal Command then sought the assistance of Bomber Command and Fighter Command. 2 Group Bostons to bomb targets on the airfield at Brest-Guipavaz and fighters to support the Sunderlands and Liberators on patrol. Both tasks involved the Ibsley wing. We, with the Exeter and Portreath Wings escorted the bombers on their raids on the Brest airfield. As the Ibsley wing had the only long-range fighters, the Canadian Mustang squadron at Middle Wallop, we were to support the Coastal Command aircraft on their patrols. Operation Instep was born. I briefed Wing Cdr Bunt Waddell, the Commanding Officer of the Mustang Squadron. We then moved the squadron west to an advance base at Predannack on the west coast of the Lizard Point in Cornwall. This was as near to the operating area that we could get the Mustangs. The Spitfires would also operate from Predannack as required. Their patrol time would be shorter than that of the Mustangs.

I flew two or three sorties with Bunt Waddell to check on the operational conditions. On information passed to the Mustang squadron in Predannack by Coastal Command we usually rendezvoused with the Sunderlands or Liberators at the Northern end of their patrol line and then stayed with them until relieved by the next section of four fighters.

There were a few skirmishes with Fw190s. We lost one aircraft and the Fw190s lost one with one damaged.

On my last sortie with Bunt we had turned north on the patrol line with a Liberator when the Allison engine of my Mustang started to make some nasty, unwelcome noises. The Liberator was flying at about 2,000ft to obtain some visibility range. Bunt and I were about 4,000ft with the other section of two at about 6,000ft. I called Bunt and told him I would need to ditch and for him to carry on but to leave one aircraft of the top section with me, temporarily for five minutes after the Liberator was well clear of our present position. The Mustang with me was to climb and call our base to fix our position and to send out the next relieving patrol early, then rejoin Bunt.

After my North Sea ditching experience I first tightened my safety straps then detached my oxygen line and radio cables. The weather was fine with a broken sky. The sea was choppy as would be expected in the Bay. We were near the northern end of the patrol line. I could see the southern coast of the Brittany peninsula and to the east, the west coast of the French mainland. As I neared the surface of the sea, as before, I pulled the nose of the Mustang up slowly and endeavoured to stall the aircraft on to the water with as little forward speed as possible. It did not float as long as the Hurricane. However, it was sufficient for me to separate and get rid of my parachute. My dinghy inflation worked this time. I opened the CO_2 bottle and the gas inflated the dinghy quite quickly. I then climbed aboard and started to survey my position. Not so good, I thought, but I was alive, at any rate for the time being. The sea was rough and waves tended to swamp the dinghy. The sky was overcast.

There was no aircraft orbiting me. It had gone as ordered to rejoin Bunt and the Liberator after calling for a fix on my position. I knew I was approximately ten miles off the French coast because that was the position of the patrol line of the Liberator that we were supporting. At sea level I could not see any land. For the time being the weather fortunately was fine with an overcast sky. However, to the West the weather looked stormy and the wind was from the west. However, it was blowing me towards land. The sea was choppy though probably as calm as the Bay ever got. Then, to the west I saw a Liberator flying south on the patrol line with four Mustangs and two Spitfires. The latter broke away and flew in my direction. Clearly they must have seen me as they orbited me and then climbed up, obviously to enable a new fix to be obtained on my position. They then flew low over me at low speed and we exchanged waves. They continued to orbit me.

After an hour or so a relieving patrol of four Spitfires arrived. These patrols over me continued without a break until dusk. I assumed the normal patrols had been briefed up to form because of the proximity of the Fw190s at Brest-Guipavaz airfield. Once, in the distance, I saw four Fw190s flying south, presumably to attempt to intercept and destroy the Liberator or Sunderland flying about. As darkness fell, the weather changed. It started to rain and rainstorms continued throughout the night. I was already wet and cold, so rain made little difference. However, under the rain clouds the wind got up and the short, choppy sea gave way to long swell. I spent an uncomfortable, wet and cold night. However, the weather started to improve soon after daylight. My watch had stopped, of course, so I only had an approximate sense of time by the position of the sun.

What seemed a long time after dawn a Spitfire patrol of four appeared overhead. They, in turn, were relieved by another four and then a Mustang appeared with a Spitfire escort of four. I found out later the Mustang had come from Portreath or Perranporth to check the situation prior to sending out a Warwick to drop a rescue boat to me. What seemed hours later a Warwick escorted by Spitfires appeared overhead. Slung underneath was a small boat. After orbiting me two or three times the Warwick, flying at about 1,000ft altitude, initially positioned itself upwind of me and released the boat. Three parachutes appeared from the boat and it descended safely to the water. As it hit the water a line shot out from each of the port and starboard gunwales. These were to help the person being rescued to reach the boat.

When I saw the lines, on the end of each was a small yellow float; I paddled towards the boat as best as I could with my hands as it drifted down to me. I grabbed one of the lines near to the boat and hauled myself, and the dinghy, close to the boat. I tethered my dinghy to the boat and with some difficulty hauled myself aboard. The boat was decked with a small cockpit at the stern. In addition to a sail the boat also had an outboard motor. Before the war I had been a small boat sailor with an international. I looked in the cabin carefully, keeping as much water out as possible. I found dry clothes including a waterproof coverall. I changed quickly and then saw a Thermos container, it was full of hot coffee from which I had two cupfuls. There was also biscuits and chocolate – I was beginning to feel human again. I stepped outside into the cockpit, closing the cabin up carefully to keep the water out, then I fitted the tiller to the rudder stem, stepped the mast and from the cockpit set the mainsail. Then I set course for Ushant and sailed round it in the dark that night into the English Channel.

My escort of Spitfires had left me, once they saw me aboard the rescue boat. I assumed they did not want to draw attention to me. Two came over just before dark, obviously to obtain a last fix in my position before dark. I was now in sight of the south coast of the Brittany peninsula. I kept about eight to ten miles out to sea. Some time later, I estimated about two to three hours, I saw what I thought were the lights of the Brest crabbing fleet and the German Navy patrol boats with them. I decided to wait a little, continue in the darkness, hopefully using the crabbers as cover. This succeeded. By first light I had rounded Ushant and was hopefully steering for the Cornish coast. As the morning wore on I was picked up by a section of two Spitfires. Thereafter, I was covered continuously by a section.

Later in the day I saw a small Naval vessel heading towards me. I hoped it was Royal Navy, if it wasn't there was nothing I could do about it. It turned out to be a Royal Navy MGB. They took me on board and took the air sea rescue boat in tow together with my dinghy. However, I said

I would like to finish the rescue in the yacht, this I did with the Navy leading me in. The air sea rescue squadron would certainly want the ASR boat back, and probably a report from me. The skipper of the MGB told me they were heading for Helston where they would put me ashore. A Spitfire escort stayed with us until dark. As we berthed alongside the wharf an ambulance drew up with a Royal Navy doctor on board. Despite my protestations that I was A1 physically, he said that persons rescued at sea had to have a medical examination when brought ashore. I agreed and said as long as I could have a bed afterwards. He said this would be provided together with food and drink. I thanked my rescuers for what they had done for me and obtained their agreement to get in touch with the Air Sea Rescue Warwick squadron concerning the recovery of the ASR boat. I would take my deflated dinghy with me.

In Royal Navy sick quarters the Naval doctor went over me physically and pronounced me fit. He then took me up to the Wardroom. We had a beer together then, after a very light meal I retired to bed. I awoke mid morning the next day, I had a shave and dressed in the only clothes I had which had been provided for me in the Naval sick quarters. After lunch, a car was sent to take me back to Ibsley.

The car went via Dartmouth where I met an old friend, Lt Cdr Luard. We had worked together when I was at Air Ministry, on aspects of the transfer of the Fleet Air Arm to the Royal Navy. He was now involved in the ferrying of agents to France and the rescue of aircrew shot down in conjunction with the French underground. We discussed the possibility of me having a trip sometime. After a drink and a meal the car was made available for me to continue my return to Ibsley. On my return I spoke with Group Capt. Arthur Vere Harvey at 10 Group and the AOC. I was told personnel from the Coastal Command and the ASR Squadron were coming over to see me. I then had time to thank the boys in the Wing who had covered me so well. We then had a party - did we have a party!

The next day I resumed the leadership of the Wing. Although the *Luftwaffe* Bf109s and Fw190s rarely reacted to fighter sweeps nowadays, we continued to do a few. It was good training for new pilots.

Our support operations of Bostons and B-17 Fortresses usually produced an enemy fighter reaction. The Bostons we were able to support all round, penetration target support and withdrawal. The B-17s we could only support as far as our fuel radius of action would allow. Sometimes we would be called upon to provide withdrawal support for RAF Bomber Command aircraft returning from deep penetration raids in early morning daylight. Occasionally fighter support on a low-level bombing raid, such as that on the Amiens prison, would come along.

On 5th March, 1943, I claimed my first victory in a Spitfire. On Ramrod 63, both 129 and 616 Squadrons, led by me, provided close escort to twelve Venturas on a raid at Brest docks. Nos. 66 and 602 Squadron provided escort cover. One Fw190 flew into my gun sight and presented me with a no-deflection shot as he tried to get on the tail of one of the Venturas. I gave the Fw190 a long burst. I hit it and it caught fire. The Fw190 then lost height. In this encounter I had to be careful that I did not hit a Ventura that was close to my firing line. In the ensuing mêlée I damaged another Fw190, as did three other members of my wing. We lost two Spitfires and four Venturas that we were supposed to be protecting. However, the Venturas claimed direct hits on the target – an arsenal in Brest Docks. My combat report for this action follows, and the Fw190s were almost certainly from JG2:-

PERSONAL COMBAT REPORT
W/C MORGAN, D.F.C.

(A) 5th April, 1943
(B) W/C Morgan leading Ibsley Wing
(C) Spitfire VC. 2 cannons/2 m.g
(D) Approx. 1740/1750 hours
(E) Over Brest
(F) No cloud. Vis. 15/20 miles
(G) Nil
(H) Nil
(I) 1 Fw 190 dest. 1 Fw 190 damaged.
(J) Nil

GENERAL REPORT

1.   Coming out of the flak approximately 10 Fw
190s attempted to bounce us. I saw two diving out
of the sun towards me. I broke left 360 degrees
and as I was regaining position I saw a further 6+
Fw 190s climbing up to attack the bombers from
below. One was getting into position to attack to the
left and below the bombers. I was approximately
500 feet above and to the left of the Hun. I dived
on him and closed rapidly from approximately 400
yards to 100 yards. I gave him one short burst 15
degrees 2/3 ring deflection. As I drew almost level
the hood and the whole side of the cockpit broke
up, and the aircraft commenced to slip slowly down
towards me. I broke right and up 360 degrees as
the Hun dived on me.

2.   As I turned I saw another Hun getting into
position on the starboard side of the bombers and
below. I completed my turn about 3-400' above him
on his port side, and afdter a quick look around,
went after him. As I closed from approximately
800 yards I saw another Hun turning in towards
me. I opened fire at 400 yards and gave two short
bursts. I missed with the first, and hit the engine
cowling, pieces of which broke up, with the second.
I broke left and up 360 degrees and saw the tailing
Hun go down very fast. I regained position up sun
of the bombers and saw two Huns above in the sun.
As one came diving in, presumably at the bombers,
I broke left into him and he continued dive away
without firing. The 1st box was escorted without
further incident,

Signed   T. Dalton Morgan   W/C

Experienced pilots in the Wing also led low level armed
rescue operations in sections of two or two sections of two.
One day, about this time, Wing Cdr Bunt Waddell led three
of his Mustangs on one of these low-level armed rescue
operations, known as Rhubarbs. They were returning low
level over the French coast when Bunt flew through a
treetop and lost part of his propeller blades. His No. 2

called to the other section of two, 'Bunt has had it'. Before
the section leader could reply Bunt called, 'Oh no I haven't'.
Bunt flew on with a badly damaged propeller, crossed the
Channel and landed back at Middle Wallop. I flew over to
see him and the aircraft. Each of the three blades had lost
approximately the same amount. The engine became rough
but held together and got Bunt home.

Sometimes the Ibsley Wing, being geographically located
in a central position, flew east to the base at Northolt or
Hawkinge and to support 11 Group Wings, occasionally to
Coltshall where 12 Group was based, or west to support the
Exeter and Portreath Wings. When the *Luftwaffe* started
their Fw190 fighter-bomber sea level raids on the English
Channel coastal towns and resorts such as Brighton,
Eastbourne, Exeter and Plymouth, we, the Ibsley Wing, put
four or eight of our aircraft at the advanced landing ground
at Bolt Head, near Start Point. Here we were located to
intercept the Fw190s. They flew at sea level and we did not
have sufficient early warning of their approach, however,
we usually caught them on the way out. This usually led to
a successful skirmish. We tried standing patrols sometimes
but they were no more successful than our cockpit readiness
at Bolt Head.

On the 21 February, 1943, a minor episode that occurred
while I had the Ibsley Wing is perhaps worthy of mention. I
had become concerned about gunnery practice for the pilots
and for myself. I had a word with the Wing gunnery officer,
Sqn Ldr Dick Durrant, and we decided to take the Tiger
Moth and look around locally for an area where we could
put up some targets. We had been taking a close look at
some ground to ensure it was not too swampy. I was coming
round the edge of a wood and in front and close to our
Tiger Moth was a power line. At the low altitude that we
were flying it was completely hidden by the wood. It was
too late to climb over, so I straightened up and flew under.
The very top of the fin caught the line and brought us quite
softly to the ground. I got out of the cockpit and looked to
see how Dickie was. He was OK and was calling that we
were on fire. I helped him out of the cockpit, I had already

seen the small flame at the top of the fin where it had hit the power line, I went over and extinguished it. There was very minor damage. The worst of the incident was that the power to the local village of Fordingbridge was cut.

During late 1942 or early 1943 we were instructed to remove the wing tips on our Spitfire Vs. This was alleged to give us additional five knots in speed but clearly would reduce the ceiling as the aircraft lifting surface would be reduced. This instruction applied to all the Spitfire Vs in Fighter Command. I had a Squadron of Spitfire VIIs with extended wings and semi-pressurised cockpits. This gave them a height advantage. On wing shows the Spitfire VIIs always flew top cover. We always used their improved height performance to our advantage. I spoke to my AOC about the instruction. I suggested as we were the only wing with some Spitfire VIIs we should not clip the wings of the Ibsley Spitfire Vs. We should be used as the top cover wing over the clipped Spitfire Vs. We were strategically located in the centre of the country at Ibsley, so that we could move east or west to provide top cover as considered necessary. The Air Officer Commanding, Air Marshal Sir Charles Steele, agreed and said he would speak with the Commander-in-Chief.

The next I heard was that I was to report to the C-in-C, now Air Chief Marshal Leigh Mallory, as quick as possible. I flew to Northolt and was then driven to Bentley Priory, the HQ of Fighter Command. Eventually I was ushered in to the C-in-C's office. I saluted, stood to attention and waited to be addressed. After a while he looked up and said, 'I didn't think you looked like that Dalton-Morgan'. To myself I replied 'like what sir?' After a pause the C-in-C went on to ask why I was disobeying his orders. I replied that I did not intend to, but before clipping the wings I thought that the special situation regarding the Ibsley Wing should be reviewed. If the Spitfire Vs in my wing also kept their wing tips, we would have at least one Wing that could provide top cover. In view of our geographical position we could provide top cover in 10 and 11 Groups as required. I left and returned to Ibsley. The next day the AOC 10 Group called me and told me the Ibsley Wing could retain all Spitfire wing tips for the time being.

Soon afterwards, in 1943, we heard that Bunt Waddell and the 400 Squadron Mustangs would leave us. We in the Ibsley Wing were sorry to lose them. They had fitted into the Wing and were popular. We had a Wing 'ding' (party) in our local, The Saint Leonards at Ringwood in Hampshire to bid farewell to them. They were replaced at Middle Wallop by a USAF squadron equipped with Spitfires. It seemed they were fresh from the USA and had come to us for familiarisation with operational procedures in the European Theatre. They would only be with us temporarily. I went over to Middle Wallop to greet them and to brief them as to what they would be doing with us. The colonel commanding this squadron appeared older, in his forties, than normally expected in those days. As I remember, he had been commanding a unit in the US National Guard. I lent them an experienced flight commander, from one of the Ibsley squadrons, to familiarise the American pilots with squadron battle formations and squadron positions in a Wing operation and on fighter sweeps. They also did some low-level armed reconnaissance in pairs and fours.

On the first practice Wing operation I had the colonel fly as my No. 2. As we were climbing to operating height I noticed he had his oxygen mask off and was smoking a cigar. I gave him a call, told him unless he wanted to go up in a fireball, to put his cigar out, put on his oxygen mask and turn his oxygen on. This he did. Our normal drill was to switch on oxygen before take-off. The Squadron did a few sweeps with us and two or three short-range bomber support operations. Their Spitfires were not equipped to carry long-range tanks. After five or six weeks the Squadron left us to eventually become part of the US Army Air Force.

CHAPTER NINE

HQ 10 Group

ON THE 12th June 1943 my time as Leader of the Ibsley Wing reluctantly came to an end. One day Group Capt. Vere Harvey, of HQ 10 Group, telephoned me to say I had been selected to replace him as Group Captain Operations at 10 Group HQ at Rudloe Manor near Bath. After farewell parties at Ibsley, Warmwell, and Middle Wallop, I proceeded to 10 Group HQ at Rudloe Manor. On arrival I reported to Air Vice-Marshal Sir Charles Steele, the AOC, who told me I could have a squadron leader to assist me. I asked if I could have Sqn Ldr Geoff Warnes, who was one of the Whirlwind Squadron Commanders. Geoff was due for a rest. The AOC agreed. I telephoned Geoff, and, like a good airman, he was not too happy about coming off flying. However, we were good friends and when I told him his Squadron was to be re-equipped with Typhoons and, after a rest, he could go back to the Squadron again as CO, he was happy.

Our job as staff officers was to co-ordinate the operations of the four 10 Group Wings, as required, and to meet overall operational plans. This involved liaison with the US 8th Air Force HQ at High Wycombe, HQ 2 Bomber Group, RAF, and occasionally RAF Bomber Command. My friend Group Capt. 'Johnnie' Walker was now the RAF liaison officer at the US 8th Air Force headquarters which made the job a little easier. At 10 Group our responsibilities included giving our Wings their tasks, timings and rendezvous as appropriate. The Wings would then do the tactical

planning. Another friend of mine was at 10 Group HQ.
He was Group Capt. Ted Colbeck-Welch, who I had not
seen since we were in 22 Squadron together, and his job
was to co-ordinate night-fighter operations for the
Group.

While I was at HQ 10 Group we were visited by
Queen Mary, the then Queen Mother, together with
two of her ladies-in-waiting. She arrived in a beautiful
1911 maroon coloured Daimler and was met, of course,
by the AOC. At this time she was living in
Gloucestershire and was involved with her ladies in
embroidering an historical tapestry. After she was
shown around the Operations Room and South West
Signals Centre we assembled for afternoon tea. As I
recall it was a glorious late summer afternoon. After
the Air Officer Commanding (AOC), his Senior Air
Staff Officer (SASO) and Chief Administrative Officer
had sat with her for a short while, each of the staff
officers was introduced to Queen Mary and rotated in
turn to sit next to her, for a brief, informal chat. I was
the last to sit by her and I responded to her questions
concerning my recent flying and when I had joined the
RAF. A wasp then flew in through the open window and
tried to join us for tea. With an imperious gesture Her
Majesty said, 'Dalton-Morgan, remove that wasp'. I
stood up, caught the wasp, first attempt fortunately,
and put it in my trouser pocket. It stung me of course
but I was graciously thanked by Her Majesty. After tea
we all went outside for a group photograph with Queen
Mary before we said farewell to her as she left in her
Daimler.

The Group HQ flight was at Colerne only a few
miles away from Rudloe Manor. Apart from the small
4-6 seater communication aircraft there was a
Hurricane used by the AOC and the SASO for their
visits to the stations in the Group. Geoff Warnes and I,
by nefarious means, managed to add a Spitfire and
Whirlwind to the flight to keep us in flying practice. As
Group Captain in charge of night operations Ted

Colbeck-Welch was able to use one of the Beaufighters in the night fighter squadron housed at Colerne. One day, SASO 10 Group was visiting stations in the Group using the Hurricane. He was flying in the vicinity of Dartmouth when he collided with one of the balloon defences in the area. In the resulting crash, he was unfortunately killed.

Later, in 1943, Geoff Warnes completed his rest from operations and rejoined his squadron, 263 Squadron, again as Commanding Officer. The Squadron had lost its Whirlwinds and was now re-equipped with Typhoons. Sometime after he had rejoined the Squadron Geoff was out on a shipping recce and was returning at low altitude between Alderney Island and the Cherbourg peninsula, known as flak alley. As he reached the northern end of the alley it appears that he was shot down. He ditched but for some reason did not get into his dinghy. His No. 2 orbited and apparently thought he was in serious trouble. The No. 2 was a young Flying Officer named Tuff. He baled out to assist his CO. Both were subsequently drowned. Two good officers were lost. The young flying officer was recommended, quite rightly, for a Victoria Cross. His action was beyond the call of duty and with risk to his own life. Unfortunately, in my view, it was not posthumously awarded.

This leads me to Geoff Warnes, a born leader who had the confidence of both his juniors and seniors. I was fortunate to have him as a squadron commander in my Wing and as my able assistant as a staff officer as well as a friend. Geoff's eyesight was not up to standard and he wore spectacles. However, he obtained one of the earliest sets of contact lenses. They were made of glass and covered most of the eye. They got Geoff through to flying but he could only tolerate them inserted for about two hours at a time. He would then have to rest his eyes for a while and use his glasses for reading. I got to know this courageous, patient and loyal officer well. He was awarded the Distinguished Service Order (DSO) and the Distinguished Flying Cross (DFC).

There was one other episode of possible interest while I was at HQ 10 Group. I had a friend, Lt Cdr Luard, who was in the Royal Navy and was the inventor of the Luard board used by the Naval navigators at the time. From time to time, we at 10 Group organised fighter cover for the MGBs and MTBs that he operated. One day, he rang and asked me if I would like to go on one of the MGB or MTB operations. I replied that I would, but that it would need to be at night because of our work. He also agreed that my assistant, who had replaced Geoff Warnes, could come as well.

As arranged, we reported at Perranporth and were met by Lt Cdr Luard who briefed us on the mission. It was to deliver one or two agents into France and, if required, bring out anyone being smuggled out by the French underground. We set sail before dark so that it would be dusk by the time we arrived off the French coast. The man, who we were told was an agent, appeared in the cabin escorted by an officer. He, the agent, had a glass in his hand and looked as though he had had a few but his appearance and dress were totally nondescript, presumably this was to help his absorption into the background in France.

We arrived off the French coast near Morlaix without incident. We had not seen or apparently had not been seen by enemy aircraft or the E boats that patrolled off the French coast and which, when I was with the Ibsley Wing, we had often attacked on shipping recces. We moved carefully among the inlets off Morlaix and then stopped. A rubber dinghy was put over the side and the agent was transhipped and rowed ashore, with the dinghy returning with five passengers. They were USAAF aircrew. After taking them aboard we moved slowly and carefully into open water and then set course for Dartmouth.

The German boats patrolled on three lines parallel

Paddy Bandon

Tangmere 1951. 'Old
Boys' of 43 Squadron.
Left to right,
W/Cdr H Wright,
TDM, 'Dizzy' Allen
and 'Killy' Kilmartin.
(via Andy Saunders)

TDM with Dee, Germany 1951.

Tan Cottage, 1952

Dee, aged
23 years.

Defence Research Establishment, Salisbury, Australia, May 1958.
TDM is sitting in the front row, fourth from the right.

Woomera. Caricatures of TDM and colleagues.

TDM sitting front row, fifth from left, in front of a Valiant bomber.

Private beach on our sheep farm at Esperance. Tom, Dee, and grandson Gwilym with our dog 'Oddball'.

Tom with sons, Gavin and John, in the shearing shed.

Tom, with grandson, admiring
the view at Esperance.

Dorothy Selway

OPEN TODAY 2-3 P.M.

BY DIRECTION OF GROUP CAPTAIN & MRS. T. F. DALTON-
MORGAN WHO ARE MOVING TO WESTERN AUSTRALIA.
By Auction on the property Wednesday, 7th April at 10.30 a.m.

BELAIR
1 ST. JOHNS DRIVE
(entrance opposite St. John's school, Sheoak Road)

**YOUR OWN PRIVATE VALLEY WITH RAMBLING FAMILY
HOME**

It comes with a whisper — not a roar — you will walk along a
seemingly endless driveway with an entrance so concealed that
it is nothing short of a miracle if you even find it — but walk you
will — and at the end of the path you see what appears to be a
thousand tall gum trees enshrining the rambling house with
Adelaide glimpsed far below almost as an ancillary happening —
you will feel the exultation of that brief shining moment — the
feeling of coming home to total privacy and oneness with
nature.
The home is unpredictable and has four bedrooms, two
bathrooms and vast rambling living areas and every room
overlooks those magnificent gums — steadfast and true — just
being there.
I hesitate to tell you of the master bedroom suite (designed for
romance) which has an en-suite like a ballroom with such unexpected luxuries as a bidet because I don't want you to run
away with the idea that it's luxurious — because it isn't — it's
just home — a home where there has been much laughter and
fun — so it is with sadness and a great deal of humility that it is
offered to you.
P.S. There are some funny old stables too.
Open for inspection tomorrow (Monday) 2-3.30 p.m. or by appointment.

How to sell a house!

Gavin 'Chunky'.

Patrick.

Our family.
*(photographs
arranged by
Vic Seymour)*

John.

Geoffrey.

David 'Chips'.

to the French coast in this area and as we were leaving the patrolled area we were spotted by an E boat that started to chase us. He fired at us but we were out of range. We started to pull away and eventually the E boat disappeared into the darkness. We arrived back at Dartmouth in morning twilight. After thanking Lt Cdr Luard for our overnight outing we headed straight back to HQ 10 Group to be in the office on time. We then checked to see if there were any changes overnight in the operational situation that might have required our action.

While I was at HQ 10 Group, there was a period when I suffered severe headaches from time to time. When a walnut shaped lump appeared on the left side of my neck I thought it best to see our septic. He sent me off to RAF Hospital Halton, the same afternoon, without giving me any indication of the problem. On arrival, I was booked in and put in a private room. There I was left for two days without attention until I called the nurse in and said if the 'septics' did not come and see me I was going to dress and go back home as it would soon be Christmas. The Senior Medical Officer then came to see me after which I was put in a car and taken off to Westminster Hospital, London.

After I was settled in a bed in a private room one of the senior consultants to the RAF, later Sir Stanford Cude, came in to see me. He examined me extensively and then said he would operate on me that night to examine the lump and remove it. The next morning, when I was in bed recovering from the operation, Sir Stanford came in to see me. He carried a plate and said something like, 'Here is a bunch of grapes for you, I picked them out of your neck last night'. I looked on the plate and saw the grape-like objects. He then said they were lymph glands that had become infected with tubercular bacteria. My chest, however, appeared to be clear. He said that he would like to keep me in for a few days and, in answer to my query, I could then return to flying. By this time it was almost New Years

Eve 1943/44. On the night I enjoyed an excellent party with the hospital medical staff and a few days later I was discharged fit for flying duties.

I returned to HQ 10 Group to be told that I was to be posted to HQ 2nd Tactical Air Force and I would be replaced at HQ 10 Group by Wing Commander Peter Brothers. I had hoped I would be able to return to operational flying.

CHAPTER TEN

2nd Tactical Air Force

I EVENTUALLY joined HQ 2nd Tactical Air Force at RAF Uxbridge. At that time there was only the Commander-in-Chief, Air Marshal Coningham, the Senior Air Staff Officer (SASO), Air Vice-Marshal Groom, and the Chief Administrative Officer, Air Marshal Smith. The staff was slowly but steadily being assembled and I was to be Group Captain Operations.

My first task was to ascertain what resources 2nd TAF would have. It was clear that there would be no new resources. Once we were firmly on the continent some of Fighter Commands fighters and fighter-bombers and 2nd Group Boston bombers would be transferred to 2nd TAF. Air protection of the invasion force during the cross-channel passage and during the initial assault would be the responsibility of Fighter Command. Thereafter, if the assault was successful and we moved forward, air support of our advancing land forces would become the responsibility of 2nd TAF.

During the assault over the beaches I was able to have initial control of the cab rank of six or eight aircraft from my Spitfire IX. This may have been because of the communication system that Jack Profumo and myself developed. As the leading soldiers called up for air support to deal with enemy tanks, a pill box or enemy holed-up in a farmhouse, I would signal two or more aircraft off the cab rank to deal with the designated targets. These aircraft would then be replaced on the cab rank by others. I was also one of the first to check out our first Pressed Steel Planks (PSP) airstrips that were built by one of our airfield construction teams in the first three days after the assault landing in Normandy. During our advance across Europe 2nd TAF either put PSP strips down as required or used captured enemy airfields.

Our first Tactical Air Force group, No. 83 Group, had formed and would now start to take over the tactical control of aircraft from the fighter command groups, e.g., 11 Group. A couple of times I went into the large room that served as a temporary ops room and found Air Vice-Marshal Groom, SASO, doing what I thought was my job. I always found him a very capable and likeable senior officer. When he had finished what he was doing I said 'With respect sir, you are doing my job, may I go back to flying?' He replied, 'No, come and get on with it, at present your job is more interesting than mine.' He left me with a friendly smile.

My main daily task, in consultation with Group Captain Ops at our tactical group – Group Capt. 'Tap' Jones – and with my opposite number in the 2nd Army HQ, Brigadier David Belchem, was to decide how our air force was to be used the next day to the best advantage for our advance into Germany. This, of course, included the use of Boston bombers in 2 Group.

After moving our advance HQ into France, behind the Army, we established our first winter HQ in Amiens, and were enthusiastically greeted by the French population. The women who cleaned our HQ would do anything for us for a bar of soap. The Army was now moving NE rapidly and we were in Brussels for Christmas 1944/45.

While at Brussels the Army conceived the operation 'Operation *Market Garden*' to capture the bridges at Nijmegen and Arnhem as a gateway into the NW German plain. Field Marshal Montgomery wanted to be the first into Germany.

The combined airborne forces of US and Britain would carry out an airborne assault on Nijmegen and Arnhem. 30 Corps, 2nd Army, would then advance up the road through Eindhoven to Nijmegen to reinforce the airborne forces as quickly as possible. General Brereton, the American general who was in overall command of the US and British airborne forces, came to our operations room early on the day the operation was to be launched, to consult with our meteorologists. Army intelligence had indicated that there was a German tank division in Laagr, a short distance from the Nijmegen bridges. This was confirmed by our Spitfire PR recon that morning. The meteorologists forecast a fine day for the initial airborne drop but conditions on Day 2 (D2) and Day 3 (D3) of the operation would deteriorate.

Despite the information on the German tank division near the bridges and the weather forecast, the decision was made to launch the airborne operation from the English bases. Our 2nd TAF fighters rendezvoused with the DC-3's (Dakotas) as they crossed the Belgian coast and supported them to the dropping zones. Withdrawal support was also given. A cab rank for base support was also supplied. On Day 1 (D1) there was low cloud over the Dropping Zone (DZ) and poor conditions at the airfields in England but a re-supply mission was able to be flown. However, the Germans had occupied the DZs and most of the re-supplies fell into their waiting hands. On D2 the UK bases were fog bound and much needed re-supply missions could not be flown from England. We now asked if we could help.

We had a few containers that could be fitted on to the Spitfires. These were loaded by the Army and dropped as designated by them. The 30 Corps advance from Brussels up the road through Eindhoven to relieve the airborne troops was also not going too well. The plan was to reach Nijmegen in three days but strong, unexpected German resistance was met nearly all the way. It took seven days for advance units of 30 Corps to reach Nijmegen.

While HQ 2nd TAF was wintering in Brussels the weekly conferences of Army and Air Force

Commanders-in-Chief began. They were to keep
General Eisenhower informed of ground and air
situations, any problems and to enable General
Eisenhower to issue any overall directives needed. I
attended some of these as staff officer to my
Commander-in-Chief, Air Marshal Coningham.
Sometimes the various Commanders-in-Chief became
somewhat competitive when presenting their reports of
operations.

On one occasion we had an unfortunate incident to
report. In one of our regular daily operational
directives 2 Group was given the target and grid
reference of a German target to be bombed. An error
was made in the grid reference at the briefing of the
bomber crew. This led to The Hague in the Netherlands
being bombed in error. This, of course, caused political
repercussions and an Air Military investigation in 2nd
TAF. We, of course, checked that we had sent out the
correct grid reference, so had HQ 2 Group, to the
bomber wing. Apparently the error was made by a
junior intelligence officer when setting up the crew
briefing material.

I do not know whether it had anything to do with the
bombing incident, but while we were at Brussels, a wing
commander, whose name I cannot recall, joined my staff
from one of the No. 2 Group Bomber Wings. When he
reported to me he said he had a car that he had captured
from a collaborator. He showed me the vehicle and I
said that if he wanted it to be fuelled and maintained at
HQ TAF it should go into the Operations Staff pool and
be used, as necessary, by any of the Operations staff.
This apparently upset him and he reported it to his
former Group Commander. Sometime later I met Air
Vice-Marshal Basil Embry, AOC 2 Group, who
mentioned what the wing commander had told him. I
told Air Vice-Marshal Embry what I had said to the
officer and he wholeheartedly agreed – that was the end
of it.

Soon after 2nd Army crossed the Rhine at Wesel that

had been flattened by our 2 Group bombers prior to the crossing. Canadian Army supported by our 84 Group, 2nd TAF, had cleared Holland and had now moved up on the left flank. The Second Army and the Canadians now moved into the NW German plain while on the right flank, General Nugent, commanding the US 9th Air Force and the US 9th Army, was also moving east of the Rhine.

About this time our second group, No. 84 Group, moved up to the left flank supporting the Canadian Army. Their task was to clear the Netherlands. This allowed 2nd Army to concentrate on crossing the A Line at Wesel, just North of the Ruhr. Our advance HQ had moved on to German soil at Aachen. We moved into what had been a mental home. In the grounds were literally hundreds, maybe thousands of nightingales that together made a disturbing noise at night, every night. Attempts to get them to move proved unsuccessful.

Since Brussels I had acquired four wing commanders. This ensured that Operations was manned for 24 hours. This was necessary for planning and liaison purposes, particularly with our adjacent US tactical air force on our right flank and the heavy bombers when we needed their support.

While at Aachen, we and 2nd Army received a visit from the Prime Minister. After lunch he said he would like to look over Germany. He was accompanied by General de Guingand and my C-in-C, Air Marshal Coningham, together with an assortment of Army and Air Senior Staff Officers. After a few minutes looking around and over the Rhine the Prime Minster called all present to piss on Germany. We all did.

In December 1944, the Germans broke out of the Ardennes, first in a last desperate attempt to capture the US Army dumps of fuel and other supplies behind the front line, and advance on Paris again. This could have succeeded. For three days as the Germans advanced, the weather, snow and low cloud prevented our aircraft from flying. Then it cleared and the fighter bombers of

General Andrews of Central TAF, supported by 9th Air Force and some of our 2nd TAF aircraft, set about the German tanks and infantry. On New Years Day the *Luftwaffe* carried out a fighter straffing raid on Eindhoven and other allied airfields. Some of our aircraft were caught on the ground but enough got off to tackle the raiders and make it an expensive operation for the *Luftwaffe*. These were the last major German air operations before fighting was terminated.

CHAPTER ELEVEN

Post War Postings

AFTER THE peace treaty was signed, 2nd Tactical Air Force became part of the British Air Forces of Occupation (BAFO), Germany. I stayed with them for a few months and then I was posted home to Staff College and later Imperial Defence College. While at Staff College I met briefly Lieutenant, the Duke of Edinburgh at the bar. At that time I assumed he was visiting us from the Naval Staff College, on matters of mutual interest – we often reciprocated visits.

From Imperial Defence College I went to the School of Land/Air Warfare at Old Sarum near Salisbury. The Commandant was Air Vice-Marshal Brown. The school was divided into two wings.

The Offensive Support Wing was led by Group Capt. 'Tap' Jones, a former colleague I had known in my previous appointment, and the Transport Support was led by another Group Captain. Courses were run in both Wings, some for middle level officers and two or three a year for senior officers, brigadiers and above. In a series of talks and exercises the students were shown how air and land forces worked together to achieve a common objective. This had been done successfully in North Africa and in the assaults and subsequent advance across France into Germany.

While I was at Old Sarum, the school was asked by the Royal Australian Air Force to send over two experienced officers to Australia for the opening of their Land/Warfare School at RAAF Laverton in Victoria. A Group Captain and myself were selected. We flew out in an Avro York via Luqa in Malta, Habbaniya, Iraq, Tenqua, Port Darwin and finally RAAF Laverton. While in Australia, apart from giving talks at Laverton, I flew a Vampire on demonstration flights around Australia. These included high entertainment in every state. I was favourably impressed by Australia and its people and decided I would one day return. Little did I know what fate had in store and I would return and spend many happy years there.

From the School of Land/Air Warfare I was posted to Special Duties. I found out I was posted to Fontainebleau, France, on to a small special staff of soldiers, sailors and airmen under Field Marshal Montgomery. The senior airman was Air Chief Marshal Robb, one of our very best airmen. My immediate boss was Air Commodore Sid Bufton, another good airman. The senior French airman was General de Chassey. I had French, Belgium and Dutch air force majors working with me. My old opposite number on the army staff, Brigadier Belchem was now a Major General and as I remember Chief of Staff to the Field Marshal. My opposite number was now Colonel Hunt who found subsequent fame by leading the first successful team to climb Mount Everest in 1953, when Edmund Hillary with Sherpa Norgay Tensing made the ascent to the peak. Colonel Hunt used to go training for the climb in the Fontainebleau Forest. Apparently some of the water worn rocks in the forest were similar to some of those found around Everest. I would, on occasion, go with Colonel Hunt to keep myself fit. We also had one Royal Navy representative on the staff and an observer for the USAAF.

In addition to the above, there was a full Colonel from the French Army who was one of the most intelligent in the team and later was promoted to general. There were also French, Belgian and Dutch Army and Air Force Staff Officers, Wing Commander Jackman, communications and one radar specialist.

This organisation became known as WEDO, the Western Europe Defence Organisation. It was put together for the sole object of producing a plan for the defence of Western Europe with existing armament and support facilities. From this organisation in later years, NATO was formed.

A plan was duly formulated and presented to our

masters. A meeting was then called at Fontainebleau with the Foreign Ministers of Britain, France, Belgium and The Netherlands to present the plan to them. The plan was presented in outline by the Field Marshal who, wasting no further time, said, 'I recommend a complete withdrawal to the British Isles in the event of a real threat'. The Foreign Ministers were obviously taken aback initially by the brevity and reality of this statement. However, they then sat down with the Field Marshal, Air Chief Marshal Robb, General de Lattre de Tassigny, Defence Chief of French Forces and General de Chassey. After a brief discussion of fifteen to twenty minutes the French Foreign Minister rose and said something like 'On behalf of all the Foreign Ministers we now direct you to draw up a plan for the defence of Western Europe, detailing the resources and deployments required'. We all then withdrew for lunch. Something that had been planned for a three-day session was concluded successfully on D1 before lunch.

I participated in the formulation of the new WEDO plan but did not attend its presentation. As always when in a staff appointment I was trying to get back to flying. Fortunately I usually managed to have a Hurricane or a Spitfire and later a Tempest to keep in flying practice. In about 1948 I was released from WEDO and given command of a Vampire Wing of three squadrons at Gutersloh in Germany. This was one of four Vampire wings on the NW German plain facing Russian occupied East Germany.

CHAPTER TWELVE

RAF Germany

MY FIRST action as Wing Leader on arrival at Gutersloh was to place myself in the hands of Flt Lt Curly Winters, the Wing Instrument Rating pilot. Curly was a likeable and very competent pilot. As Wing Leader I wanted my green ticket, which was the highest rating one required for flying in the most adverse weather conditions. I obtained my ticket fairly quickly. At the same time I was putting in time on the Vampire and getting to know my squadron commander and pilots.

One of the tasks as a Wing Leader was to see that my squadron commanders were doing their job to train their pilots up to as near combat standard as possible. This included air-to-air and air-ground firing on the range at Sylt on the North West German coast. This was popular not only because of the live firing practices possible, but because the beaches adjacent to the firing ranges were full of nude and near-nude young lovelies in the summer. These could be viewed at leisure returning from firing practice. I also kept myself up to date in firing practice. Our wing strength training was often helped by simulating an enemy force raiding Britain, and providing exercise for the air defences. On one of these exercises one of the squadrons taking off on the shorter runway at an advance airfield in The Netherlands lost a young sergeant pilot. This aircraft struck a pole when just airborne with a little airspeed and he crashed and was killed. Both the squadron commander and myself had used and checked the suitability of the runway for a wing take-off prior to the exercise. If the aircraft had taken off in sections of two instead of sections of four or the pole had been noticed earlier, the accident may have been avoided. The pole was too near the end of the runway.

We also flew north to Gardermoen airfield in Norway to participate in joint exercises with the Norwegian and Swedish air forces. One day, when it was time to return to Gutersloh, the weather was not suitable for the whole wing to return. So with the squadron commander I selected eleven pilots who were up to green ticket standard. The weather en route would mean an above cloud flight all the way. The weather at Gutersloh was cloud base 800ft, visibility about one mile. It was an excellent opportunity to test our weather flying as a formation. I briefed our Senior Air Traffic Officer, Flt Lt 'Dickie' Dickson and our Ground Control Approach (GCA) Officer. I set up our checkpoints and alternative airfields. Finally, I briefed the selected pilots. I left one squadron commander at Gardermoen to bring the remainder of the Wing home when the weather was suitable. Twelve of us, including me, then took off and set course for Gutersloh. We climbed through solid cloud to 20,000ft and flew over cloud the whole way. About 100 miles out I contacted Dickie in the tower and called for a homing to base. We were not far off course. Over base we came under GCA control. I put the other two sections of four aircraft in line astern about 800yds apart. GCA then brought us down to finals. We broke cloud at about 800ft, visibility about a mile as forecast, then made finals and landings as individual fours. A successful flight that we repeated as our pilots became trained up to standard. It was a confidence building exercise as well as a test of skill.

It was while at Gutersloh that I met Dee, who was later to become my wife. Dee's first husband had been shot down and killed whilst flying a Boston on a raid to destroy a railway depot at Lille. Dee's second husband was one of my fellow officers at Gutersloh and, in spite of us both loving the same women, he remained a good friend to both of us. Dee and I fell in love – really in love – and we are still in love fifty years later!

Unfortunately my private life was in an emotional mess as I had married at the outbreak of war and, like many wartime marriages, it did not last.

Towards the end of the war my father had died and, sadly, I could not attend his funeral as the Crossing of the Rhine operation was about to start. And when, in early 1945, my brother John was shot down over Germany I was devastated. His body was never found but his name is on the Runnymead Memorial.

Looking back at this stage I missed a home to go to. My mother had died when I was young and this had made my brother and I very close, now he was gone.

Over the course of the war I had met a number of women that appeared to love me. I am afraid I invariably hurt them and for that I shall always be sorry.

Now here I was at Gutersloh, doing what made me happy, flying! Meeting at last the only woman I have ever really loved but who, unfortunately, was married to someone else. Instead of sorting out my problems, I was creating more.

Dee and I went to see Paddy Bandon – Air Marshal the Earl of Bandon – who was the senior air officer, and confessed everything. He was a great friend to both of us and remained so until his death. He was also a man of the world.

During our talk he peered over his glasses at us and pointed out that we both had to stop and think. His parting words were, 'If you love each other so much, and I think you do or you would not have come this far, you are in for a rough time'. Well we were but, fortunately, we came through it all even more in love.

Paddy Bandon and his wife visited us twice in Australia while he was C-in-C of the Far East and was delighted to see us settled and prove him right.

As my tour as Wing Leader at Gutersloh came to an end on 5th November 1951 I was promoted to command the Wunstorf base nearby. The Wing Leader there was Wing Commander Powell. There were also 1000 German prisoners of war on the base awaiting release. I used them on the base farm, for keeping the runways and road around the base clear of snow and ice. They also helped with the more menial tasks around the base. We RAF worked through their officers and NCOs when detailing tasks. The military way was the most acceptable and best way to get things done. While I was at Wunstorf the British High Commissioner for West Germany issued a directive that we could now fraternise with our former enemy. We invited their officers to the Officers' Mess and NCOs to the Sergeants' Mess. The airmen fraternised freely. This was good for relations and co-operation.

Wunstorf was a good base. Formerly it was a permanent *Luftwaffe* base and had many recreational facilities. These included the Steinhuder Lake, adjacent to the base, for sailing and swimming.

While I was at Wunstorf our Army of Occupation arranged a large military exercise on the NW German plain. The Wunstorf Wing participated in the exercise. In the Officers' Mess we had a luncheon for Field Marshals Montgomery and Slim and their staff officers. After lunch my C-in-C, Air Marshal Sir Harry Broadhurst asked me if I would fly Field Marshal Slim over the exercise area. He would like to see it. I had our two seat Meteor made ready for flight. Like a similar aircraft at Gutersloh this one was normally used for instrument flying training, pilot check flights and refresher flying as necessary.

After supervising that the Field Marshal was correctly strapped in I climbed into my cockpit, taxied out and took-off. It was a fine day, good visibility and a broken cumulus cloud base at 2,000ft. This and the warm sun caused the ride to be a little bumpy. We reconnoitred the exercise area at about 1,500ft altitude, going lower to observe items of particular interest. Towards the end of the flight the Field Marshal reported that he was not feeling well and slightly airsick. He used the bag provided but had slightly marked his uniform. He did not want to land at Wunstorf with a stained uniform. Could I help?

I called up my old base at Gutersloh and asked Dickie (the efficient and friendly Senior Flying Control Officer), told him the problem without mentioning the Field Marshal by name, asked Dickie if he would get one of the batwomen down to the tarmac immediately with water, towels and an iron. In the meantime we flew into Gutersloh. The two

young women cleaned up the Field Marshal's jacket very
quickly. It was now unmarked, the girls had done an
excellent job. We then took-off and headed back to
Wunstorf. After landing the Field Marshal thanked me as he
had done to the girls at Gutersloh. Later in the day my C-
in-C asked me if I had landed anywhere. I told a white lie,
but I felt that he sensed that I had. Field Marshal Slim did
not want Field Marshal Montgomery to know he had been
slightly airsick.

I had two good officers and friends to help me while I
was at Wunstorf. Wing Commander 'Killy' Kilmartin, who
was my Administration Officer. He had been one of my
flight commanders in 43 Squadron and we had known each
other since we were very young officers. Also Wing
Commander Jackman, my Engineer Officer who was the
most efficient, helpful and friendly officer you could wish
for.

When I left Wunstorf in 1952 I was posted back to
England pending my release from the RAF to take up a more
lucrative post with the British Australian Project in
Australia. I went to the North Weald sector in Fighter
Command and I was based at Trimley Heath under Air
Commodore 'Ronnie' Lees, an Australian. When he was
posted his successor was Air Commodore Smith, a South
African. He had been on night fighters. Again, I found them
both most helpful to me, efficient and pleasant to work for.
Life here was quieter and more relaxed than in Germany.
We were all keen flyers and sometime airborne in the two
Hurricanes visiting the operational units. It was from
Trimley Heath that I was released from the RAF in
November 1952.

CHAPTER THIRTEEN

Woomera

I COULD now start to plan a firm future for Dee and her children and myself. It would be some time before I would take up the appointment in Australia. So I needed to look around for something to do. We had just moved to a house at Frinton-on-Sea. One Sunday night in early 1953 there was a very bad storm on the East coast. Heavy rain and strong winds, and on the Monday morning we heard on the radio that high seas had breached the protective dykes along the coast. Dee and I had by now our first son, David (Chips). Volunteers were being called for to help make emergency repairs to the dykes. I reported to the person who appeared to be in charge. To start he put me sand bagging with some other volunteers.

Later I found out he was the engineer-in-charge of the repairs, provided by the construction firm who had been given the task of making emergency repairs, then temporary repairs and then the final permanent dykes. I got to know him when we sat down to rest or when eating our sandwiches. The Salvation Army were soon on the scene as usual, looking after us. One day I was sitting down with Mr Austin, the engineer-in-charge, and by this time we had got to know each and like each other. He asked me if I would like a job with the firm and to work with him on the project. I explained that eventually I would be going to Australia but in the meantime I would like a job. He said that this would be satisfactory but added that he hoped that eventually I might like to remain with the firm. I stayed with the firm for most of 1953. I worked long hours, seven days a week, was well paid and learnt a great deal about construction work. I set up a local servicing bay for machinery, e.g. diggers and caterpillar tractors and allocated them as required and according to forecast weather conditions along the coast. Mr Austin even trusted me to do the pay run sometimes!

Frinton-on-Sea was a delightful spot where even the buses were not allowed to drive through the town. In those early post-war years the parties at the Grand were fabulous. One weekend we were invited to a Fancy Dress Ball by the hosts, Bobby and Sally Anne Howes of 'showbiz' fame. We arrived in fancy dress but, much to my disgust, Dee had dressed me as a pirate (shades of Henry Morgan) while she was elegantly dressed as a Victorian lady. On our arrival – a little late – the fancy dress parade had ended and everyone had changed into formal evening dress. Dee looked fine but I looked like a barbarian trying to make my knives and cutlass less conspicuous! I vowed I would not go to another Fancy Dress Ball again – and never did!

Whilst at Frinton we were visited by the parents of Monty Cotton, an Australian who had been in 43 Squadron. They brought with them two Australian nursing sisters who had made the journey to England to receive medals from the Queen. One of them, Vi Bullwinkle, had been in a group of nurses that had been machine-gunned down by Japanese soldiers. Seeing the first nurse shot she had the good sense to fall down and was left for dead with the others. She survived the war, being hidden by various villagers and scarcely eating. They remarked, during afternoon tea on our tennis court, 'We didn't think we would ever live to sit in an English garden eating cucumber sandwiches.' Brave women indeed.

Shortly after we moved to Tan Cottage at St Osyth as the location was more convenient for me to travel. The cottage was owned by the South African High Commissioner and was built originally in the 14th century. It was charming and Dee and the children were able to enjoy a holiday there before we sailed for Australia.

The sailing date had to be delayed as Dee was expecting our second child. Our lovely daughter, Carol-Anne, was born and our sailing date set for February 1954. So now we

had a family of five. Dee's eldest son, Patrick, came home
from Chard School in Somerset to join Athalie and Geoffrey
together with our own Chips and Carol-Anne.

Friends and relations came to say good-bye and a convoy
set off to take us to Tilbury where we were to board the SS
Orsava on her maiden voyage.   After long drawn-out
farewells we boarded and were shown to our cabin while
the children were taken to their four-berth cabin. Our cabin
was festooned with flowers, telegrams and cards and I was
amazed that people I had not seen since the war had taken
the trouble to wish us well. There were telegrams and cards
from my fitter, during the Battle of Britain, Bill Littlemore,
43 Squadron and even Paddy Bandon to name but a few. To
our further delight Dee noticed an envelope from P&O,
who owned the ship, and thought it might be an invitation
to have drinks with the captain. When it was opened we
saw that it contained a cheque refunding us one-quarter of
the fare. Apparently workmen would be travelling on the
ship to finish off the ballroom and other areas. They would
be working at night and the line hoped that we would not
be inconvenienced.   Finding another cheque in the
children's cabin we rang the steward and ordered a bottle of
Champagne. This surely was a bloody good show and an
auspicious start to our new life.

The weather was fine and grew warmer as we sailed
south towards the Mediterranean. We put into Naples for
twenty-four hours where we went ashore. We then sailed on
to the Suez Canal. It was an interesting experience to sail
through the Canal and down the Red Sea. Each day we
played deck games, swam in the pool and lazed in the sun.
Part of the time the baby and young children were looked
after and played in the nursery. It was a holiday for all of us.
As we sailed south down the Indian Ocean it became hotter
as we approached the Equator. There were celebrations as
we crossed the Equator and initiations for those who were
making the crossing for the first time. I had crossed twice,
but in the air.

After we had reached the southern tip of India we headed
northeast to Colombo, Ceylon. Again we stayed here

twenty-four hours. We all went ashore except the baby. Dee and I visited one of the many jewellers and I bought her a ring. The owner became very friendly towards us as we browsed around his shop. Eventually he drew me aside and asked me if I would deliver a parcel for him to a friend in Australia. Dee and I discussed this and eventually declined as we laughingly thought he might be sending drugs, especially when he offered to halve the price of the ring.

Back on board ship our convivial life continued. We were having a good time. One night as we approached Australia we passed the Royal Yacht *Britannia* conveying the Queen home, after her Coronation visits to Australia, New Zealand and the South Sea Islands dependencies. Both the *Britannia* and the *Orsava* were well lit up and be-flagged. We had a ball and toasted the Queen and had a wonderful firework display. Eventually we put into port at Perth, Western Australia. Here some passengers disembarked. While here we had a surprise phone call from the parents of a Monty Cotton (Bush) whom had been in my squadron. We were invited to sail on around to Sydney and stay with them at Palm Beach where they were holidaying. As there was some time before I would take up my appointment we accepted gladly. Otherwise we would have disembarked at Adelaide. However, we did have time to catch a first glimpse of Adelaide that eventually would become home to us. We also called in at Melbourne on the way to Sydney. That reminded us both of a provincial English city.

We then set course on the final leg of a memorable and enjoyable voyage of Australia. It was a fine warm day as we entered the beautiful harbour of Sydney through the North and South heads. As it was the maiden voyage of the *Orsava* we were met by a fleet of small sailing and motorboats and a cacophony sound from ships in the harbour and some of the buildings on shore. We then sailed under Sydney Bridge then made for the Pond O berth at Circular Quay where we tied up. The voyage was over and a new life was about to start. After disembarking I left to see about our luggage. Dee told me later that she stood surrounded by the children looking at the *Orsava*. It was her last connection with

England. She felt very sad and must have been showing it. One of Australia's tall and muscular wharfees in his blue vest came up to her with a pint of tea and said 'Drink this lovey, it will make you feel better'. Always after this Dee championed the wharfees whenever they went on strike, which they often did.

After I returned to Dee we were met by Mr and Mrs Cotton. I then collected our luggage from Customs. Then we were whisked off to Palm Beach by the Cottons. Here we had a most enjoyable introduction to Australia, swimming, sunbathing and children playing on the beach over the next few days. Then we were driven up to Oberon, some 100 plus miles west of Sydney, not far from the Blue Mountains. Here we were put in a guesthouse, about one mile from the town centre. The house was located on a hillside and surrounded by pleasant countryside. We were visited and entertained by the Cotton family. Their business was the cutting and milling of timber from the local forests and railing it to Broken Hill for use in the mines.

The business was run by the eldest son, Robert, who later became Sir Robert when he became the Australian Ambassador to America. The second son was Monty who had been in my Squadron when I was CO and was an excellent pilot. Mr Cotton the Elder treated me in every respect like one of his sons. We arrived at Oberon at a late Easter in April. Soon after we arrived I was plunged into the celebrations of my first Anzac day. While I was there I accompanied the firms field supervisor, Stan, and observed the selection of trees for cutting, which was done in conjunction with the New South Wales Government forest rangers. The selected trees were cut and stripped by cutters employed by the mill and the logs transported to the mill in the firm's trucks.

During our stay at Oberon I kept in touch with the Weapons Research Establishment, now known as the Defence Research Establishment, concerning my appointment. I was eventually given a date to arrive in Adelaide, South Australia. For a family the journey from Oberon, NSW, to Adelaide, South Australia, was a little

complicated. It was before the days of air travel. We were
taken by car to Parks. There we transferred to a train that
took us to Broken Hill. Here we had to change stations for
the train to Adelaide. Dee's and my eldest boy Chips was
nearly left behind at this station. How, we do not recall. As
the train pulled out of the station we saw this small boy on
a tricycle riding down the platform waving happily to us.
We stopped the train and got him aboard. On arrival at
Adelaide we were met by Mr Brian Rofe, from the Weapons
Research Establishment Australia (WREA), with whom I
would subsequently work for a while. We were shown to a
guesthouse in a salubrious part of North Adelaide where we
were given a flat. We eventually bought a house at Glenelg
by the sea and I had twelve happy years here where we had
four more children, Suzanne Jane, Gavin Andrew, Sally
Anne and John Roderick, making our family nine children.
We also acquired a wonderful nanny, namely Mackie (Mrs
Matthews) who had been a riverboat stewardess and more.
She was with us for almost twenty years until she remarried.
I gave her away and Dee was her bridesmaid, remaining
friends with her until she sadly died.

The next day I was picked up by car and driven out to
Salisbury to the WREA. Here I was introduced to the
Director and Deputy Director and met Bill Watkins with
whom I would work initially in Mathematical Services
Group. This was a Group that would analyse all the
telemetry, time theodolite and photographic etc. records of
tests conducted at Woomera. Bill was an excellent person to
learn from and work under, and friend. As part of the
learning curve I was eventually transferred to Missile
Projects Group run by another excellent person, Jeff
Heinrich, who also became a good friend. It was to MP
Group that a potential Ranger User would first submit his
requirements for conducting tests at Woomera, particularly
the precise information he required from the tests. MP
Group would then appoint a Project Officer to work with
the Range User and prepare the instructions for the conduct
of the tests at Woomera. This was then sent to Woomera for
the conduct of the tests in conjunction with the appropriate
Range User.

The word Woomera is aboriginal and means spear launcher. Its choice for the Australian Range was very appropriate.

After I had been at WREA about nine months the Deputy Director called me in and asked if I was ready to go to Woomera as Officer in Charge of Range Operations. I replied in the affirmative, but indicated I would not take my family mainly because of education problems. I asked could I normally fly down to Adelaide Friday pm and return to Woomera early Monday am as did the Range Users. This was agreed. If tests continued into a weekend I would of course stay at Woomera. I proceeded to Woomera on this basis. Jeff Heinrich had just gone to Woomera as the Superintendent of the Range. This was a good arrangement as I had already worked with Jeff in MP Group at Salisbury and we got on well together.

Woomera was now becoming a large complex. The campsite was growing into a modern village of about 5,000 inhabitants and all facilities, shops, bank, cinemas, swimming pools, radio and later television. Adjacent to the village was the technical area that supported both the Range and the village. It contained a first class airfield including hangars. This served the Monday to Friday air service to and from Adelaide and the helicopter and fixed wing aircraft flight that supported Range Operations.

The Range Head was some twenty kilometres northwest of Woomera village and the Technical area. It comprised the Test Control Centre, the launchers, test shops where missiles and vehicles were finally prepared before being moved to the appropriate launcher, the target aircraft airfield and dangerous stores area and a small administrative supporting area that included a canteen. Nine launch areas were located some 200-400 metres in front of the Test Control building. Two launch areas for the large European Development vehicles were being built out on piers extending out on salt lakes near the Range head. The Range centre line extended on a heading of 340 degrees across Australia to the West Coast between Port Headland and Broome. The Range extended twenty kilometres each side of the centre line and after some 100 km down range narrowed towards the centre line. Time theodolites, cameras, radars and telemetry stations were deployed on each side of the Range centre line to cover the flight of missiles and launch vehicle tests from launch to impact. Operators were flown in and recovered each day by helicopter to man the appropriate instruments station for a test and recovered again afterwards. There were thirty-six cattle and sheep stations on the Range that were connected by telephone to the Test Control Centre for them to receive firing warnings as appropriate. Each station was also provided with a shelter. Some were also connected to the Range centre line road that gave them access to the Woomera village facilities.

The topography of the Range is generally flat. Occasionally 'theatre' salt lakes and hillocks of sand. The vegetation is mainly stunted bush. When it rains uncertainly every few years in the centre, the desert blossoms with flowers. Each of the stations on the Range extended for kilometres. Most raised sheep and a few cattle. I visited the stations regularly to maintain our good relations, inspect our communications and the shelters that had been installed for the homesteaders. Generally, they were friendly, reliable and co-operative people. Mrs Green of Purple Dawn station asked to keep her homemade goodies in her shelter. There was still room for her and the family.

Turning to the operation of the Range, the heart of the Test Control Centre was the Test Control Room. This contained all the facilities for the Test Control Officer to co-ordinate control and conduct a test. To assist him he had a Test Safety Officer who controlled the firing circuits to add the launchers. He also issued preliminary and imminent firing warnings to the appropriate homesteads so that they could take shelter. He also had an Instrumentation Control Officer who kept him aware of the state of the instrumentation in use and co-ordinated operation of all instrumentation for a test. The Trials Control Officer also had a direct inter-communication link to the Range User in the test facility below each launcher. At each launcher we also had a Launch Safety Officer who monitored all actions on the launcher and who was linked to the Test Safety Officer in the Test Control Room. Alan Mole was our excellent and regular Trials Control Officer. Occasionally, in his absence he was replaced by myself. For his outstanding efforts Alan was awarded an MBE.

Adjacent to the Test Control Room was the Plotting Room. This of course was also linked to the Test Controller. It was also linked to the complex. The Plotting Room had four horizontal plotting tables. These were for plotting the vehicle under test and for plotting and controlling target and launching vehicle aircraft to the appropriate interception positions and timing required in a test. Initially the Royal Australian Air Force (RAAF) provided the staff to maintain and operate the unmanned target aircraft system. However, the RAAF needed to withdraw the personnel for normal aircraft duties. So we contracted the task out to Short Bros who operated a similar target system in Llanbedr, Wales for the missile Range at Aberporth. He had two excellent aircraft controllers, Rod Polkinghorne and Don Neadham. I supported them as necessary. Later they were joined by an RAF officer. Flt Lieut Ben Pampline was also first class. From time to time I also assisted with aircraft controlling.

The target aircraft flight consisted of the small individual unmanned aircraft specially built for the task and Meteors and Canberras converted to the unmanned role. Testing the latter two aircraft for unmanned flight gave me an opportunity to fly. I also learnt to fly the helicopters at Woomera. The Jindivik was designed and built in Australia as a small unmanned target aircraft. It was used for most of the tests that required a target but that did not require the destruction of the target. The unmanned Meteors and Canberras were resolved for this role. At the conclusion of a series of trials a missile would be fitted with a warhead and fired against one of these aircraft to demonstrate its lethal effect.

I also had a recovery team. The team leader was Lieut Cdr Percy Hawkins; he had a team of six assistants. His task was to search for and locate, if required, take photographs of any missiles in the impact area that a Range User wanted after a firing. The Range User would accompany the Recovery Team for this purpose. He also had to clear the Range of any remaining debris. It was in our mandate that the Range had to be kept clear. When Percy retired he was replaced by Sqn Ldr Don Tungate.

Our Native Patrol Officer, whose name I cannot recall but he was an excellent person. The Range crossed a large native reserve in the centre of Australia. The Native Patrol Officer carried out the necessary liaison with the Aborigines to ensure that they were safely clear of any missile impact area during a firing. We used the helicopters to support him. During the Maralinga nuclear tests our tasks were to ensure a large area around ground zero was clear of aborigines and to provide the meteorological information required. We would never say the designated area was absolutely clear. We could say that to the best of our knowledge it was clear. It was very easy for an aborigine to hide in the desert bush when ground and air recces were in progress. In fact a few did!

Mr Brookman was our explosives and dangerous stores officer. Not only was he responsible for storage until such items were required on a launcher but for keeping the Range clear of such items as unexploded bombs.

The types of missiles developed and tested at Woomera included air-to-air missiles, air to ground missiles, ground to air missiles and ground-to-ground missiles. Early development of these missiles before the Woomera range test took place in Britain, Australia, France, and to a lesser extent America. The aircraft launching air-to-air and air-to-ground missiles operated from Woomera airfield, Edinburgh airfield adjacent to WREA and sometimes as far away as RAAF Richmond in Victoria.

In addition to missile development, rocket vehicles were fired into the stratosphere and outer space carrying experiments seeking data for various universities and research institutes. Some 460 of these vehicles were fired, most during my tour at the Range.

Some larger British and US vehicles were also fired. These carried, for example, fuses for nuclear stores for test during re-entry. The European Launcher Development Organisation (ELDO) fired nine vehicles. Seven were fired along the Range centre line with various degrees of success. The last two were fired in a northerly direction. The first stage landed in the Simpson Desert, the second stage in the Gulf of Carpentaria and the third stage in the ocean north of Papua New Guinea. To maintain a check of these two vehicles, radar was deployed at Gove on the Gulf of Carpentaria. I was involved in the calibration of this radar before each test. This required that I flew to Darwin and then 400 miles east to Gove. During these trips I made my first personal contact with our original Australians. One young brave with whom I became friendly showed me the skill with which he could launch a spear. I saw him hit the trunk of a tree about 18-cms in diameter at about 80 metres range.

Back at Missiles Group at WREA Salisbury, Adelaide, the weekly programme of tests and the detailed instructions for tests were prepared. These were then sent to the Range. Here they often needed to be modified, for example because of an overhang on the previous week I issued a daily 'programme' that reflected any changes. Similarly the test instruction would be amended to reflect any Range User or rang Authority changes agreed since the test instructions were issued. The Range could handle up to about twenty-seven tests a week depending on the requirements for the tests. Usually it was sixteen to twenty, not more.

Up to three trials involving targets could be programmed in one day. In the summer, because of the heat, tests commenced at 0600 am. The time allocated for each test allowed a reasonable time for delays that occurred during the countdown on most tests.

After three enjoyable and energetic years at the sharp end, my tour at the Range came to an end. I had seen the build up and the peak of test activity. I returned to Missile Projects Group at the Weapons Research Establishment at Salisbury, South Australia. Here I would meet with a potential Range User to ascertain the information he would require from tests at Woomera. Then with our instrumentation specialist examine whether or not we, the Range Authority, could meet his requirements and if not, what additional instrumentation would be needed and if and when it would be available. A Project Officer would then be appointed to work through detail with the Range User and prepare the detailed instructions for the test(s). One of my tasks was to coordinate and progress the activities of the Project Officers. I would also continue to liaise with the Range User as appropriate. I also set up a small operations room at WREA Salisbury to facilitate monitoring of Range activities and for liaison with RAAF Edinburgh, particularly when tests of air-to-air and air-to-ground missiles were being mounted from there. This operations room was run by one Dick Alderton. We also had a Draughting Section in Missiles Projects Group under Bob Gordon. Among other things this section did any work required by the projects and by the Range User. On my visits to the Range, Bob often accompanied me. This helped to familiarise him with Range requirements. The activities of Missiles Projects Group were coordinated by a Principal Scientific Officer. After Jeff Heinrich went to the Range I eventually took his place as Principal Officer Missiles Project Group.

My job at Missile Projects Group took me from time to time on visits to the UK, USA and France. These were mainly for preliminary discussions with potential Range users or with users of the Woomera Range. In the UK I sometimes visited the Range at Aberporth, Wales where the Range Controller was a Welshman, Dai Davies. This Range was very restricted, but allowed preliminary firings into Cardigan Bay before they came to Woomera. Indirect targets were flown from Llanbedr located near the coast in the centre of Cardigan Bay. My visits to the USA sometimes included a visit to their Range at White Sands in Mexico. This range was saturated with work and they were pleased to find out that we had time to spare at Woomera to help them. Thereafter there was nearly always a US project at Woomera. On one visit two of us were staying at San

Bernadina near Los Angeles. Our discussions were with a potential Range User in Los Angeles. On this visit I had three brushes with the police - none unpleasant. After I left the firm I was working with, one day I went down to Rivers, a few miles from Los Angeles, mainly to visit the university. While I was there I looked around the shops to find a present to take home to my wife. I was angle parked in front of some shops where I had been browsing. I was about to get in to my car when two motor cycle police patrol men drew up, one each side of my car. They came up to me and said I had been reported by one of the shopkeepers for what to him was 'casing the joint'. I explained I was a visitor from Australia and showed my diplomatic passport and opened my briefcase. They were then most helpful and pleasant.

On the same visit to US at the conclusion of my business I was driving up to see Lake Arrowhead before returning to Australia. On the way I pulled into an open piece of land to eat my sandwich lunch. While there, some motorcyclists came and parked about 100 yards away from me. They changed into cowboy clothes and careered around the area firing six-shooters. The firing must have attracted some police attention. Up came two police motorcycle patrolmen and tackled me first. Did I have a gun? Despite my answer in the negative and seeing my passport they searched the car and my briefcase. I explained where the firing had been coming from so they headed in that direction where the 'cowboys' were now sitting down to eat. Without ado I then left for Lake Arrowhead. The Lake and its environs were magnificent.

I am glad I saw Lake Arrowhead before I left the US. On the third occasion I had pulled aside on the freeway on my return to San Bernadino for a rest. I fell asleep and was awakened by a policeman tapping the window. After showing my credentials he told me the location I was in was not a safe place to stop and he recommended a place further on. I then continued on my journey.

The return flight to Australia was via Hawaii. There were six of us in first class. Three of them worked for the Teamster Union in the US. One was the nephew of the

Union Leader who was in gaol. He was accompanied by his wife and son. They all worked for the Teamsters Union. They were going to Hawaii to raise support for the Challenger for the Presidency in the next election. They were pleasant people and we had a small party on board.

While I was at Woomera we, of course, had several official visitors from Britain, Australia, America and France. Among these was Air Marshal Elworthy. He came while we were testing the first British air-to-air missile. This was a beam rider. The range of the missile was 3,000 yards and the pilot would need to hold the beam on the target for fifteen seconds. We watched some of the firings together. I commented to him that I could not visualise a pilot in combat maintaining straight and level for fifteen seconds. Air Marshal Elworthy agreed. This missile never went into service. However, it probably served to introduce the RAF to air missiles.

One of the more onerous tasks that fell to me as Chief Range Authority Planner for the tests was to cost them. This was particularly difficult for tests in early development phase, where unforeseen delays could lead to the extension of range time and additional tests. A contingency allowance of twenty-five percent in the costing was not unusual. The Americans naturally wanted a costing of their tests before they arrived. This was difficult, as we often did not have the information we needed for a costing until they arrived for the tests. However we usually worked through these difficulties.

Each day at the Range started with a visit, discussion and briefing at the Meteorological Bureau located in the Technical Support area adjacent to the village. The head of the local bureau was one George Trefrey. A most professional, likeable and helpful man. We also had a Met Station about halfway down the Range that provided the Woomera station with advance supplementary information. George Trefrey would attend briefings if a new series of tests were involved. Otherwise, the met briefing and discussion was usually handled by the Duty Forecaster. If there were night tests another briefing would be held at a convenient time before the night trial.

The weather factor was vital to most tests. Photographic instrumentation particularly prescribed cameras for a test would be divided into those that were essential and those that were desirable. So a test could precede the weather conditions only allowed essential instrumentation, usually time theodolites and other high-speed cameras to track and photograph the missile and provide missile position and altitude in formation. The statistics in my monthly report to my Superintendent Jeff Heinrich usually indicated that the Range Users' missile/vehicle caused most delays and postponements. The weather was second. Range instrumentation and target aircraft were usually third or fourth with the least deleterious effect on test progress.

Most days after the conclusion of trials the Range User and we would return to the Senior Mess in Woomera village and discuss the days activities at the bar. If there were night trials to follow, the Range staff and I would stay at the Range and eat in our canteen near the Rangehead at Koolymilka.

One night at Woomera when we were setting up to launch a Black Knight vehicle there was a most unusual incident. I was in the Control Room talking to Alan Mole who was setting up for the countdown to launch. A call came for me over the intercom from Percy Hawkins, our Recovery Officer, who was down range near the expected impact areas of the Black Knight and launch vehicles. He reported a very bright light that was heading towards the Range head. I stepped out on to the balcony of Test Control building followed by Alan Mole and others.

Sure enough we soon picked up a very bright light heading at high speed towards the Rangehead. It appeared to be at about 5,000ft. As it orbited around us, we could see what appeared to be a circular outline of the vehicle. A cabin protruded from the top of the vehicle, it was brightly lit and showed up the circular outline of the vehicle. As it passed behind us it accelerated and climbed away, almost vertically, to the East and disappeared. No sound came from it. The apparent circular shape of the vehicle, its speed, rate and angle of climb were beyond that of known aircraft of the time. Our Rangehead radar failed to pick it up. I reported the incident immediately to RAAF HQ in Canberra to RAAF Base Edinburgh and to Defence Research Establishments. It was seen by our Recovery Team down range and by at least six of us at the Rangehead. I would say that it was one of the three percent of such sightings that could not be easily explained away.

My final task at the Defence Research Centre Salisbury was to clear and close down the Range as it was organised and operated at that time. In the future if a missile range was required the Range User would provide and operate all the facilities he required. The Royal Authority would only continue to provide safety supervision and meteorological information.

Concluding my tour at Woomera and what had now become the Defence Research Centre at Salisbury, Adelaide, I spent twenty-seven years in the system. I always found the work challenging and interesting. It was never boring. I was sorry to be retired at the mandatory age of sixty-five in 1982. I was given a farewell party by the whole establishment and a gift. Only a few months later a Parliamentary Bill was passed stating that age would not be a mandatory reason for retirement. Bugger!

Suzanne.

Carol Anne.

Our
Wedding
Anniversary.

Sally.

Athalie.

Imperial War Museum, September 2000. A group of Battle of Britain pilots in front of a Spitfire.

The Queen Mother's 100th Birthday Celebrations. *Left to right*; Pete Brothers, Paddy Barthrop, TDM, Frank Carey, Christopher Foxley-Norris, Ludwig Martell, Wallace Cunningham, Ken Mackenzie and Pete Parrot.

TDM coming out of Westminster Abbey, 2002, after a memorial service for the Battle of Britain.

TDM and Dee meeting HRH the Prince of Wales. Pete Brothers is on the Prince's right.

Queen Mother's 100th Birthday Celebrations. I share a vintage car with Ronnie Hay, distinguished Royal Marine fighter ace of WWII.

Reunited with the old insignia at Tangmere Museum, 10 September, 2003.

Signing prints at the Aces High Gallery.

Dee at the Christopher Foxley-Norris Memorial Wall, Capel Le Ferne, Folkestone 2006. Appropriately pointing to Tom's name. *(Seymour)*

TDM *(second from right)* standing in front of a Hurricane with other Battle of Britain pilots, including Paddy Barthrop on far left.

TDM *(far left)* with Dame Vera Lynn and Battle of Britain pilots.

TDM sharing an umbrella with Luftwaffe ace Gunther Rall as they enter the Aces High Gallery.

Dee and TDM at the Memorial for Battle of Britain pilots.

Dame Vera Lynn and
Dee,

The German Luftwaffe
belt buckle and the
'half-crown'
referred to in
Appendix 7.

CHAPTER FOURTEEN

Retirement

RETIREMENT, what a gastly thought, it certainly did not help that Dee was still librarian at a High School and with a weekly book talk show on television. I insisted, selfishly when I look back, that she took early retirement so that we could start a new adventure together.

At this time one of our sons, Gavin, was the Veterinary Officer for the Agricultural Branch at Esperance in Western Australia, and our youngest son, John, was halfway through his Veterinary Science degree at Murdoch University in Perth. We went to visit John and, on the way back, had a holiday at Esperance where Gavin showed us a property for sale. It was a perfect location, underground water, a private beach and, as he pointed out, we could raise sheep for the Eastern market (he was the Vet that passed them at the port) and also breed sheep for wool. I felt it was a new challenge and something that Dee and I could do together.

The selling of the family home was difficult for Dee. However, the girls were all married, one in England, two on the land in Australia and one in Melbourne. Our sons were also established with Patrick, an Economist in Sydney, Chips at a hospital in Alice Springs, Geoffrey was the Chief Librarian at Brisbane University, Gavin a Veterinary Officer at Esperance and John at University. This was our retirement venture and I had a feeling that it would be fine.

Within a short space of time we were packed and off to Esperance. The drive from Adelaide took two days and two nights across the Nullabear. When we finally arrived at Esperance we realised that we had taken on a very big task. First we had to build a farmhouse as there was only a large 'weekender' on the property. The former owner lived in Esperance and had a manager, who was single, who only needed small living accommodation.

Then we had to build a shearing shed and all the attendant outbuildings needed for a sheep farm. Miles of fencing needed attention as one side of the property bordered on Cape le Grande, a big wild life, National Park. The other side bordered Art Linklater's property, although we never saw him during our time there.

Life was certainly different; we were an hour's drive from Esperance, a small country town, and not a neighbour for miles. However, we both enjoyed every aspect of it. Our son supplied the expertise, we hired casual labour for the really heavy work and Dee and I did all the 'everyday' tasks. We were up at dawn, as it got very hot later in the day, and I would drive round on the 'Ag' bike – a motorcycle adapted for the land – with Dee on the back checking for any problems, like distressed or dead sheep and lost lambs. We would also check the water troughs and the boundary fences as the kangaroos had a tendency to kick holes in them. Mending fences, on properties in the Outback, is an endless task and always with you for no sooner than you finish you have to start all over again from the beginning. It was not unusual for Dee to take an orphaned lamb back to the homestead and feed it from a baby's bottle. On some occasions we had as many as six lambs being hand fed.

Around our property were herds of wild horses – a wonderful sight as they always moved together with their manes streaming out, free and wild. They often broke through our fencing and a party of horse-catchers would come at the weekends and ask permission to round them up. They were hard men, excellent riders and with endless interesting bush stories. However, after a few visits Dee found out that they sold some of the wild horses for dog and cat meat. They were told that they would no longer be welcome and we would be withdrawing our permission to catch our lovely wild horses.

How different it was when the Aboriginals came to the homestead to ask permission to shoot kangaroo for food.

Here, indeed, was a lesson for our society for they never took more than they needed to eat. There was no senseless killing as the kangaroos were part of their background and 'dream-time' – something we have never understood. They would always call to thank us, often with a dead kangaroo, dripping blood, hanging around their necks and offering us a leg. After declining Dee would insist upon giving them a gift of some sort, but never an alcoholic drink as we believed that this was ruining their culture. Instead of learning from these free people who are by nature nomadic and, before the white man arrived, moved around in tribes, living in one place for a while, then burning all their rubbish and leaving the land to recover. They lived off the land and followed their 'dream-times'. The white man, with his greed, has ruined a race of people who could have taught us so much.

Meanwhile our farmhouse was completed and the shed ready for our first sheep shearing – what an experience! When the shearers had arrived one had brought his father, a small, wizened looking fellow with legs so bowed I thought what the hell use is he going to be?

How wrong I was proved. He was a New Zealander, a 'Top Gun', and could shear three sheep before the others had finished one. He had come along to help and to meet these crazy 'Poms' who had suddenly thought they could be sheep farmers.

I watched the team start and as the sheep were sheared the fleece was thrown on to a table (an art in itself) and cleaned of all the burrs that had attached, it was then packed into a woolsack. Whilst this was going on a lad, who was training to be a shearer, was sweeping up the 'dags' (the name they gave the clumps of wool that had fallen to the floor). I naturally wanted to help and, when I offered my services, the top shearer gave me a broom saying, 'You sweep up mate and release a man for shearing.' I knew my place, as I was obviously not a Top Gun here, and ended up packing the fleeces into the woolsacks.

Later, over a beer, I was told, 'The boss doesn't usually help in the shed but just looks in to see if we're working quickly enough. But we don't mind you hanging around –

you're True Blue mate!' I took this as a compliment as these men were hard, tough, salt of the earth Australians.

In the meantime Dee had been busy, she was more in demand than me as the shearers had 'smoko' at 10.00am, which consisted of tea, hot scones and a smoke. Another smoko break at 1.00pm where stacks of meat sandwiches, fruitcake and pints of tea were provided. Again at 3.00pm and finally at 5.00pm when light food and beer was taken. Dee had to drive from the homestead to the shed with all the food and drink in the back of the utility vehicle. It seemed a never-ending process as the shearers had a timetable that was strictly adhered to, 10.00am, 1.00pm, 3.00pm and 5.00pm, and if you were late with the smoko there was trouble. We had heard that the shearers walked off the job if the food was not good enough!

We enjoyed having a drink with them at the end of each day, what stories they told. On the last day they expected beer and pies laid on for a farewell party.

We had made many friends during our time in Esperance and some have remained friends. They included the local doctor and his wife, the accountant who now lives in England. Pete Smith, a very experienced farmer, who was a great friend and family man. He and his wife Christine made our time in Esperance much easier with their ever ready help and advice. We certainly needed lots of both.

We had settled down very well, starting to make money, joining the local social scene and thought we were set for life.

Our son, Gavin, had meanwhile married Anne, a lovely English girl from the Scilly Isles. She was a very competent horsewoman and travelled around to all the gymkhanas – she and Dee had much in common.

Then came the bombshell – Anne wanted to go home to England. In addition, our youngest son, John, had decided that he wanted to travel and did not want to become a sheep farmer. We realised that we could not run the place alone and, despite all our friends offering to help us out, sadly sold the property and were on the move again.

Before making up our minds as to our next course of action we decided to have a three-month holiday at Alice Springs to recover, lick our wounds and start again. Our son, Chips, was at the Alice Springs Hospital and had always been very close to us both – over the years he had become not only a dear son but also a good friend. We had enjoyed good times together, skiing at Gornegrat in Switzerland, holidays at the club in London, and sailing at the Robe Yacht Club in Australia. We were very upset to leave the property at Esperance but Chips helped us start planning again.

The 'Alice' is a place that anyone visiting Australia should experience. While there we met very many interesting characters, wonderful artists that included an outstanding Aboriginal, and doctors who were researching complaints suffered by the Aboriginal children. We also met quite a lot of 'drop-outs' from society – but still interesting. I shall never forget the Alice.

We decided to go back to South Australia and made for Robe, a delightful fishing village similar to those in Cornwall. We had spent many summer holidays here with the children as it was a tourist's paradise and, with its excellent golf, bridge and yacht clubs, not to mention restaurants, it was a pleasant haven in the winter. I should also mention that it had a very good pub called the Caledonian, which was established by Courage Brewery. Years before it had attracted the poet Adam Lindsay Gordon, the 'wild Colonial boy' and true bushman whose memorial statue is in Westminster Abbey.

Soon after moving to Robe we bought a house and settled down to our new life. We realised, however, that we both needed something more that golf and bridge after our active life on the sheep farm. One evening the Town Clerk, Rob Kay, called in to see Dee and told her that the chief librarian of the town's library had decided to leave and that they were quite desperate. Would Dee run the library until a replacement could be found?

The following morning Dee went to the library and was quite surprised when I turned up half an hour later. Thinking I could help I volunteered to put books away on the shelves.

Robe Library had a terrific Historical Centre, which needed a lot of updating and I soon found myself deeply involved and interested in the local history. Six weeks later the Council

offered Dee the position of Chief Librarian and, as I had
become interested also, she accepted. We both believed we
would be there until we were ready to retire.

There followed the most interesting and happy eight years.
The library became the social hub of the village; we served tea,
coffee and, for a small donation, a glass of wine. The summer
visitors (usually about 10,000) just loved to call in and browse
at the bookshelves with a glass of wine in their hand. In the
winter, with the pot-bellied stove roaring away, we often had
to push members out at closing time.

I thoroughly enjoyed the book buying expeditions and
when the library became computerised Dee was delighted to
have me around. The Council also seemed pleased not least
because they were getting two for the price of one! Dee's
enthusiasm and efforts to turn the library and Robe into a
literary and arts centre won her many awards from both the
Tourist and Library Boards.

Near neighbours of ours in Robe, who became good
friends, were Michael Parker and his wife Jean. Mike had been
equerry to Prince Philip, with whom he had served in the
Royal Navy, and many a night was spent talking of the 'old
days' in England over a few bottles of good Australian wine.

There are two occasions that stand above all others in my
memory of this time and one was when we were trying to raise
money to restore the lovely old building belonging to the Robe
Institute, the centre of the town's activities where dances,
wedding receptions, school 'break-up' parties, not to mention
the town's bridge club, were held. It also housed the National
Trust Art Gallery.

Mike Parker offered us a considerable number of his own
paintings saying that if we sold a few we could keep the
proceeds for the Institute. He was a very talented artist and
had produced some very fine land and seascapes.

Dee, with her usual enthusiasm, organised an art show and,
getting out the 'Whose Who', sent invitations to many people
in Melbourne, Sydney and Adelaide. Needless to say the event
made the art columns of a number of papers and all of Mike's
paintings were sold.

The other event of memory was the 150th Anniversary of

Robe, which happened to fall in 1988, the year the Tall Ships were sailing to celebrate the founding of Australia in 1788.

Mike Parker went to England as he was in charge of the board that would select the crews that would man the ships. During a meeting that the British Prime Minister, Margaret Thatcher, attended, he requested that the *Endeavour* and the *One and All* be allowed to call in at Robe for their 150th celebrations. Mrs Thatcher demanded to know where Robe was, but agreed with the board that they could have the ships.

When Mike arrived back in Robe he had already decided that as part of our celebration events we should have a dinner for 200 at the Institute with pre-dinner drinks at the library. All the stops were pulled out and we all worked jolly hard to ensure that it all went off successfully. Many of the Australian dignitaries, including government ministers, members of parliament, foreign attachés, etc., turned up and we had to turn down some MPs who tried to 'muscle' in. The whole thing was an outstanding success mainly due to the efforts of Mike, Dee, Rob Kay – the Town Clerk, the Quinlan-Watsons – a prominent family in the area, and the Robe Yacht Club.

In early 1990 I received a letter from Sir Christopher Foxley-Norris who aroused my interest with the news about the intended celebrations in England for the 50th Anniversary of the Battle of Britain. Dee, who loved England and had never become an Australian, was determined to take me back home. Little did I realise that this would be the beginning of yet another era in our lives.

We eventually ended flying in the Australian Prime Minister's (Bob Hawke) plane. The reason for this was that the Australians were providing twenty RAAF boys to be the Guard of Honour at Buckingham Palace for three days during the 50th Anniversary. So, instead of sending a half empty aircraft, the Australian Battle of Britain pilots and partners, together with those of us that lived in Australia, were offered the spare seats. This also included reporters from the Australian papers and an extremely nice chap from *Jane's* – the military magazine – who, on the flight, became an admirer of Dee, which made for loads of laughs.

Our group consisted of Air Vice-Marshal Ray Fennel (C-in-

C of the RAAF) and his wife, Air Vice-Marshal Sir Ronnie Lees and wife, Wing Commander Ian Bayles and wife, Flight Lieutenant Charles Palliser and wife, Wing Commander John Greenwood and wife, Squadron Leader Geoff Pitman and wife, and Wing Commander Powell and his wife.

It was a party from the time we left Sydney and congratulations should be given to Squadron Leader Ken Llewellyn – a serving officer with the RAAF – who was responsible for the total organisation. He still remains a dear friend of both Dee and myself.

On route to England we stopped off in Hawaii where we stayed in the Hilton Hotel for three days. Another three days were spent at the Sheraton Hotel in Winnipeg, Canada, and then on to Washington, in the USA, where we received a wonderful reception. Finally arriving in London for yet another wonderful reception and a never to be forgotten two weeks of festivities during which three major events highlighted the re-union.

The first was the fly-past over Buckingham Palace. All the Battle of Britain pilots and their partners had to assemble below the balcony where the Queen and the Royal Family were watching.

Sitting next to Dee and me was 'Cocky' Dundas, whom I had not seen for forty-five years. I always had the greatest respect for Cocky who was a most humorous and likeable chap. We did a lot of reminiscing whilst waiting for the show to start.

What a magnificent display the boys put on. At the end of the display, after the lone old Hurricane and Spitfire had flown by, a most unusual happening occurred as if it had been planned – to a huge cheer from the crowd three wild geese flew overhead in perfect formation. At this point Cocky Dundas wiped his eye and remarked, 'That must have been that bastard Bader – he 'shat' in my eye, he never did like me!'

The second event was the Dinner Dance at the Savoy and organised by Paddy Barthrop for the Battle of Britain pilots and partners. I felt a little apprehension at meeting all my dear old friends, as I know many people were disappointed when I left the RAF and went to Australia. However, this was all dispelled when we walked into the Savoy. At the top of the stairs was dear old Foxley-Norris and his lovely wife Joan. When he saw me he came down the stairs, embraced me and said, 'Welcome home dear boy, you have been away far too long.' I shall never forget this and was most moved.

When I met up with Fred Rosier (now Sir Frederick), 'Killy' Kilmartin, Pete Brothers, Frank Carey, John Cunningham, Brian Kingcombe, and many more, I felt I was home once more,

We all packed the floor and danced and sang to all the old favourite wartime songs – what a night to be remembered.

The third event was at Westminster Abbey where we paid tribute to all the pilots and crews who did not come back. I remembered my brother John, who was never found and is another name on the Runnymead Memorial. Dee remembered her first husband Pat, shot down over Lille in 1943. There were many, many memories in the Abbey that day.

After the service we were all invited to a Royal Garden Party where, once again, many battles were re-fought, many more planes shot down, many old friendships renewed and gallons of Pimm's drunk.

We returned to the hotel to prepare for our flight back to Australia. At dinner, that evening, Dee looked at me and told me that she wanted us to come home to England to live. I had half expected this and I realised this was also what I wanted. Can you wonder why my favourite song is 'On the road again', by Willie Nelson?

During our years in Robe we made many friends, including retired farmers, business people from Melbourne and, especially, those people that made up the wonderful fishing community. Leaving the village and the library, with all our friends, was a wrench. But we visit once a year as some of our children are still there. Our beloved youngest son John – a dreamer, zoologist and part vet., who absolutely loves dogs, and daughter Sally, a nurse, who lives in Adelaide. Carol in Melbourne, Suzanne who runs a winery called 'Punter's Corner' near Robe in South-East Australia, Geoffrey, a sensitive thinking man, who is also a good friend to me, is

Chief Librarian at Brisbane University, Patrick, an economist, is in China at the University of Beijing and our dear oldest son Chips is Vice President of 'Eye Care' in Vancouver. He has spent a lifetime taking care of the under privileged and we are very proud of him. We also have a daughter, Athalie, who lives in Australia, and son, Gavin, who has a veterinary practice in, Devon, England. I also have a son, Anthony, from my first marriage and was brought up by his mother. When I met him, after fifty years, I found his mother had done an excellent job.

So here we are back in England. In 2000 we had moved back here for a while and were living in Buckdon when we received a phone call from Rick Taylor of Aces High, asking if we would join them at the Duxford Air Show for the celebrations of the 60th Anniversary of the Battle of Britain. I was to be meeting enthusiasts and signing prints for them in the Aces High marquee along with other Battle of Britain veterans. I have to say it all sounded a little strange to me but Rick was very persuasive so I agreed – little did I realise that this was to be the beginning of yet another chapter in our lives.

After a fantastic weekend, meeting wonderful people and realising that Rick and his partner Colin Hudson were genuine and passionate about what they do, we were invited to their huge gallery in Wendover in Buckinghamshire. Dee immediately fell in love with the place and not one to do things by half, within months we had upped sticks and moved to Wendover where Dee and I became a regular fixture at the gallery. I spend many hours there, signing prints for the boys and meeting their collectors and it is amazing to me to think that at my time of life there is still a part for me to play.

Having started my book whilst in Australia I decided to get it finished and my dear friends Rick and Colin have given me an office with all the facilities I need, where I sit at the time of writing. Each morning I kiss my darling Dee goodbye, come to the office then I pop home for lunch and then back in the afternoon for more writing – it's just like the old days.

The office I have has a big glass door and Rick had a sign saying 'Group Captain Tom Dalton-Morgan' put across the top. One day a new customer was in the gallery and Rick asked if I would come out and meet him, which I did for a brief chat. As I returned to my office the customer turned to Rick and said 'is that the gaffer?' to which Rick replied, 'oh yes, he's keeping his eye on me.'

The years Dee and I have spent in lovely Wendover are extremely happy ones. Rick and Colin have become part of our family and the Air Shows, the signings and meeting lots of R.A.F friends I had not seen since the war is wonderful. Most of all the interesting people who I meet at the Gallery mean I have made many new friends and we never dreamed that we would have yet another chapter in the last years of our lives.

However as I look at the thousands of people of all ages, from five to ninety, who come through the gallery doors what comes to mind is something that is very important to all of us who lived through the war. The one thing we all dread is that the sacrifices that were made, especially by our many fallen comrades, will be forgotten but all of this is helping keep it alive. As I see enthusiasts bringing their young children to meet us and have photographs taken with us, it gives me hope that generations to come will still understand what we did and will remember the sacrifices of many to secure their way of life.

These people wish to keep the history of England alive and as someone once said "A nation without history has no future".

I consider myself a most fortunate man. The Battle of Britain, my years in the RAF, the flying, Woomera, Esperance, Robe. The many dear friends – some still alive but a hell of a lot killed. My wonderful children, grandchildren and great grandchildren and, best of all, fifty-two years (so far) with my lovely Dee, the only woman I have ever really loved. What a wonderful Life!

In Memoriam

Group Captain Tom Dalton-Morgan DSO, OBE, DFC*
1917-2004

Oh, I have slipped the surly bonds of earth
And danced the skies on laughter-silvered wings;
Sunward I've climbed, and joined the tumbling mirth
Of sun-split clouds...and done a hundred things
You have not dreamed of...wheeled and soared and swung
High in the sunlit silence. Hov'ring there,
I've chased the shouting wind along, and flung
My eager craft through footless halls of air.
Up, up the long, delirious, burning blue
I've topped the windswept heights with easy grace
Where never lark, or even eagle flew.
And, while with silent, lifting mind I've trod
The high untrespassed sanctity of space
Put out my hand, and touched the face of God.

Pilot Officer J Magee

Memorial Service
Adelaide, 27 September 2004

Chip Dalton Morgan   **Eulogy**
Midge Scantlebury   **A Poem**
Carol Thornton   **A Poem**
Susan Hood   **Ecclesiastes 12: 1-7**
Gavin Dalton-Morgan (UK)   **Some thoughts**
Sally Anne Cowan   **Shared thoughts**
John Dalton-Morgan   **Some thoughts**
Geoffrey Dalton-Morgan   **Some thoughts**
Sue Lewis

Leadership
Do you have what it takes?
By Capt. Eric Mold

(This article appeared in 'Dockwalk',
a Canadian Yachting magazine.
Issue: December 2000)

MANY years ago, when I was a young air force sprog, I had the good fortune to serve with a Wing Leader I have never forgotten, his name was Tom Dalton-Morgan. Tom was a real Top Gun. Runner-up to Wing Commander Johnny Johnson with the greatest number of 'kills' in World War II. He had an awesome charisma. When he entered a crowded room you could feel his presence. You did not have to see him or hear him speak to know he was there. Some sort of special aura seemed to surround him. The cacophony of conversation seemed to drop and then resume a few decibels lower when he came in. And then a small enclave would automatically open up in the middle of the room, at the point where Tom usually gravitated. Soon the previous hubbub returned with Tom holding council in the middle of it. He was the envy of the rest of us and, if it was a social occasion, the idol of all the young ladies present.

Picture a tough, stocky 5' 10" thirty something person. At one time he had played international rugby for Wales. He had an interesting, handsome face, slightly scarred by burns and his chin bore a faint imprint of a GGS gun-sight, which were souvenirs of an earlier Spitfire crash. An unruly head of fair hair and penetrating, blue eyes atop a chest full of very significant medal ribbons and you will have a picture of TDM. A young colleague once remarked 'If he said we are going to fly through that mountain and come out the other side, I think I would go with him.'   That was the kind of leadership Tom exuded. He was the epitome of leadership, he was a born leader.

There are other born leaders, chaps like Nelson, Drake and Chris Columbus that are well known to us all. The reason they stand out so much in history is because of the things they lead their men to achieve. But those that are truly 'born to lead' are very few and far between. However, all is not lost for us lesser mortals. In the intervening years I have taken more than a passing interest in the subject of leadership; reading many books by great leaders and studying their contemporaries on TV and other media. My conclusion is that I do not think it possible to become a leader of the same calibre as our great heroes but it is possible to significantly improve our leadership skills.

Comments from some of Tom's contemporaries

Group Captain P O'Brian, DSO, DFC

'(Tom) was a special individual for whom I had the highest, top admiration, and great enjoyment too during the short time we worked together.'

Group Captain George Westlake, DSO, DFC

'I was on Course 17, Staff College, Bracknell, with Tom and in my opinion he was the outstanding member of the course, and I believe he would have gone right to the very top in the Royal Air Force.'

Air Chief Marshal Sir Fred Rosier, GCB, KCB, CBE, DSO, OBE

'It would be impossible to overstate Tom D-M's importance and influence on the conduct of fighter operations for and beyond D-Day.'

Interview with Bill Littlemore

(Tom's fitter during the Battle of Britain)
March 2002

I LEFT St Athans Training School in the early part of 1940 and, shortly after, was posted to 43 Squadron who were based at Wick in Scotland. I soon settled in with a great crowd of people under the command of Squadron Leader George Lott. We got some very good experience of interception of Heinkel 111s, which were frequently raiding Scapa Flow and other targets. It was the opportunity to test our procedure and get the aircraft into the air as quickly as possible.

We then moved south to Tangmere to replace No. 1 Squadron who had been sent to France. At Tangmere we changed our procedure to each pilot having his own aircraft and specific ground crew to look after it. Tom Morgan was posted to us from the Air Ministry and took over 'B' Flight. We were fortunate to be allocated Tom who was a very good pilot. It was a pleasure to watch him land a Hurricane where it was a 'three-point' landing every time. Tom, and experienced pilots like Fred Rosier, would report mechanical problems but would also tell you how to cure them. The Squadron did a lot of convoy patrol work in the early days over the English Channel. Then Dunkirk happened and we temporarily lost Jim Hallowes. It made quite a difference to a night out in Chichester, which was full of 'Army Boys' who didn't rate the 'Brylcream Boys' who hadn't been within their view but, of course, our lads were patrolling inland and, very often, at a high level. One night in Chichester we were confronted by a group of Welsh guardsmen, one of whom unsheathed a bayonet and swung at me. If I hadn't ducked I wouldn't be here now! I got back to base and had a word with Tom and said that there was probably going to be a lot of trouble and I think somebody should get on to the Provost Marshal and make him aware of the possibility of trouble. Tom obviously acted upon my information because a couple of days later they separated the RAF boys from the army in Chichester. With Dunkirk over we quickly got back into the routine to intercept raids from enemy aircraft and one thing we tried to do all the time was to get the aircraft off as quickly as possible.

There was a routine that became fixed because one of the hold-ups was the pilot and his parachute. In the early days the pilot would struggle out to his aircraft with his parachute over his shoulder, climb into the cockpit and get settled in – all this was time wasted. The obvious answer to this was to place the parachute in the cockpit with the harness draped either side. When the alarm went the mechanic would jump into the cockpit and start the engine. He would then jump out on the starboard side. Tom by this time would have reached the aircraft, climbed in and put the parachute straps over his shoulders. I would then tap him on the shoulder to indicate that Tommy Poole, the second fitter, had removed the starting trolley cable and had pulled the 'chocks' clear. I think the quickest take-off we ever did was about 48 seconds from the time of the 'Scramble' bell. It was always a competition between 'A' Flight and 'B' Flight to get the aircraft off as quickly as possible.

One particular day I felt very fortunate as it was my turn to get the 'WADs' (rolls and sandwiches) from the NAAFI van that used to pull up between No. 1 and 2 hangers. I went a little earlier than usual and had left the NAAFI wagon at 12.45pm. and took the short-cut across the grass rather than around the perimeter back to 'B' Flight dispersal. All our aircraft had taken-off at 11.40am. and so we were expecting them back shortly. I had just dished up the WADs to the lads when there was a 'kerfuffle' over the tannoy and one of the lads said that it must be the boys now. I said that's not ours, that's 'Jerry'! I went to the door of our dispersal hut and looked up. There was a Stuka pointing his nose and with the bomb just leaving it. That was the one that landed between No. 1 and 2 hangers and killed that young lad who is buried in Tangmere Cemetery.

Thereafter it was all mayhem and it was at that precise time that I saw three Hurricanes, and an additional isolated one, approach us from the south. The lone Hurricane seemed to be in trouble and was leaving a white trail behind it – possible glycol. It approached the East-West runway an pointed his nose down so steeply I thought he was going to impact. At the last minute he pulled up, landed on the grass and came to a stand-still – unfortunately the aircraft was in flames. The pilot was Billy Fiske of 601 Squadron and was the first American pilot to be killed in the Battle of Britain.

We never really did settle down after that.

By the 30th August, 1940, the pilots and ground crew were pretty exhausted. We would go on 'readiness' in the mornings and this would continue throughout the day. Sometimes we would get the aircraft off six times in a day. I think our worst day was 'Black Saturday' – the 7th September. On that day we lost Caesar Hull and Dicky Reynell, who had just received a letter to return to Hawkers where he was a test pilot. The letter came a little too late to save him. The following day they took us out of the battle and the Monday they flew some of us up to Usworth in a York aircraft while others went by train. We were supposed to have an easier time at Usworth but we worked just as hard as we did at Tangmere.

We did a lot of coastal patrols and night fighting, at which, of course, Tom was very good. When you consider the lack of 'aids' we had in those days he must have been a pretty good pilot.

The time came when I went for further training and left 43 Squadron in late January 1941. Of the many postings I had during World War II I never found the camaraderie that existed in 43 Squadron. There was a very close relationship between the pilot, his rigger and mechanic. The idea of the pilot starting an aircraft up disappeared early on. The amazing thing about those Merlins was although they were basically identical each engine had its own idiosyncrasies. You could start it first time with a very small throttle opening. On another one you would give a couple of bursts on the primer pump, whereas on yet another you wouldn't need any. As a result of this, until the ground crew took over and actually started these engines, a pilot who was unfamiliar with a particular engine had difficulty in starting.

They were great days and it is something I would not have missed for anything.

NB. Regrettably Bill Littlemore passed away within a month of giving this interview.

APPENDIX 1

TDM's Honours & Awards

Distinguished Flying Cross	6.9.1940
Bar to the Distinguished Flying Cross	30.5.1941
Companion of the Distinguished Service Order	25.5.1943
Officer of the Order of the British Empire (Military)	14.6.1945
Mentioned in Despatches	1.1.1946
American Silver Star	
American Bronze Star	
American Distinguished Flying Cross	
Norwegian War Cross	
Belgian Croix de Guerre	

APPENDIX 2

TDM's 'Victory' Claims

Date	Aircraft/A/C	No.	Unit	Mission Time	Aircraft	C	P	D	G
3.7.40	Hurricane I	P3784	43 Sqdn	15.33-17.30	Do17			1	
12.7.40	Hurricane I	P3784	43 Sqdn	15.40-16.10	He111	1*			
13.7.40	Hurricane I	P3973	43 Sqdn	09.05-10.05	He111	1*			
21.7.40	Hurricane I	P3972	43 Sqdn	14.10-15.55	Bf109	1			
21.7.40	Hurricane I	P3972	43 Sqdn	14.10-15.55	Bf109			1	
8.8.40	Hurricane I	P3216	43 Sqdn	15.45-16.50	Ju87	1			
8.8.40	Hurricane I	P3216	43 Sqdn	15.45-16.50	Ju87		1		
8.8.40	Hurricane I	P3216	43 Sqdn	15,45-16,50	Bf109	1			
13.8.40	Hurricane I	P3972	43 Sqdn	06.25-06.50	He111	1			
4.9.40	Hurricane I	V7542	43 Sqdn	13.00-13.50	Me110	1			
4.9.40	Hurricane I	V7542	43 Sqdn	13.00-13.50	Me110	1			
6.9.40	Hurricane I	V6542	43 Sqdn	09.00-09.50	Bf109	1			
6.9.40	Hurricane I	V6542	43 Sqdn	09.00-09.50	Bf109			1	
5/6.5.41	Hurricane IIb	Z3150	43 Sqdn	11.45-12.25	Ju88	1			
5/6.5.41	Hurricane IIb	Z3150	43 Sqdn	01.25-02.15	U/I	1			
7.5.41	Hurricane IIb	Z3150	43 Sqdn	01.10-02.10	Ju88	1			
8/9.6.41	Hurricane IIb	Z3265	43 Sqdn	01.25-02.45	Ju.88	1			
10/11.7.41	Hurricane IIb	Z3265	43 Sqdn	00.15-10.05	He111	1			
24.7.41	Hurricane IIb	Z3145	43 Sqdn	15.50-16.30	Ju.88	1*			
2.10.41	Hurricane IIb	Z3310	43 Sqdn	21.15-21.55	Ju.88	1			
1.12.42	Spitfire V	EE625	Ibsley	16.30-17.45	Bf109			1	
5.4.43	Spitfire V	EE625	Ibsley	16.55-18.25	Fw190	1			
5.4.43	Spitfire V	EE625	Ibsley	16.55-18.25	Fw190			1	
14.7.44	Spitfire IX	MK782		16.00-18.15	Fw190				2
20.7.44	Spitfire IX	MK782		12.00-14.40	Fw190		1		

*C-Confirmed   P-Pobable   D-Damaged   G-Ground   Shared victories **

Battle of Britain Facts & Figures

**Royal Air Force fighter operational strength,
August 31, 1940**

On strength	Available for Operations
1,181	764

**Luftwaffe operational strength against Britain,
August 1940**

	Establishment	Strength	Serviceability
Close reconnaissance	120	95	80
Long-range reconnaissance	126	100	71
Fighter	1,011	934	805
Heavy fighter	301	289	224
Bomber	1,569	1,481	998
Dive-bomber	348	327	261
Ground attack	40	39	31
Coastal	94	93	80
	3,609	3,358	2,550

Source: Luftwaffe Quartermaster General, 6th Abteilung returns.

RAF Fighter Command Order of Battle, September 1940.

10 GROUP

92 Squadron	Spitfire	Pembrey
213 Squadron	Hurricane	Exeter
87 Squadron	Hurricane	Exeter (B Flight, Bibury)
238 Squadron	Hurricane	St Eval
247 Squadron	Gladiator	Roborough (one flight)
234 Squadron	Spitfire	Middle Wallop
609 Squadron	Spitfire	Middle Wallop
604 Squadron	Blenheim	Middle Wallop
56 Squadron	Hurricane	Boscombe Down
152 Squadron	Spitfire	Warmwell

11 GROUP

17 Squadron	Hurricane	Debden
73 Squadron	Hurricane	Castle Camps
25 Squadron	Blenheim	Martlesham
257 Squadron	Hurricane	Martlesham (B Flight, North Weald)
249 Squadron	Hurricane	North Weald
46 Squadron	Hurricane	Stapleford
222 Squadron	Spitfire	Hornchurch
603 Squadron	Spitfire	Hornchurch
600 Squadron	Blenheim	Hornchurch
41 Squadron	Spitfire	Rochford
79 Squadron	Spitfire	Biggin Hill
501 Squadron	Hurricane	Gravesend
111 Squadron	Hurricane	Croydon
72 Squadron	Spitfire	Croydon
66 Squadron	Spitfire	Kenley
253 Squadron	Hurricane	Kenley
1 Squadron	Hurricane	Heathrow
1 Squadron	Hurricane	Northolt (RCAF)
303 Squadron	Hurricane	Northolt (Polish)
504 Squadron	Hurricane	Northolt

601	Squadron	Hurricane	Tangmere
43	Squadron	Hurricane	Tangmere
602	Squadron	Spitfire	Westhampnett

12 GROUP

74	Squadron	Spitfire	Kirton-in-Lindsey
264	Squadron	Defiant	Kirton-in-Lindsey
85	Squadron	Hurricane	Church Fenton
302	Squadron	Hurricane	Church Fenton (Polish)
64	Squadron	Spitfire	Church Fenton (B Flight, Ringway)
611	Squadron	Spitfire	Digby
151	Squadron	Hurricane	Digby
29	Squadron	Blenheim	Digby
616	Squadron	Spitfire	Coltishall
242	Squadron	Hurricane	Coltishall
266	Squadron	Spitfire	Coltishall (A Flight, Wittering)
23	Squadron	Blenheim	Wittering
229	Squadron	Hurricane	Wittering (B Flight, Bircham Newton)
19	Squadron	Spitfire	Duxford
310	Squadron	Hurricane	Duxford

13 GROUP

3	Squadron	Hurricane	Castletown
232	Squadron	Hurricane	Sumburgh (one flight)
145	Squadron	Hurricane	A Flight, Dyce
			B Flight, Montrose
605	Squadron	Hurricane	Drem
65	Squadron	Spitfire	Turnhouse
141	Squadron	Defiant	Turnhouse
615	Squadron	Hurricane	Prestwick
607	Squadron	Hurricane	Usworth
610	Squadron	Spitfire	Acklington
32	Squadron	Hurricane	Acklington
54	squadron	Spitfire	Catterick
219	Squadron	Blenheim	Catterick

Luftwaffe Order of Battle in the West, September 1940.

LUFTFLOTTE 2 (Holland, Belgium & Northern France)

Aufkl.Gr.122 Stab
Long-range reconnaissance
   1./(F)22   Do17, Me110
   2./(F)122   Ju88
   4./(F)122   Ju88, He111, Me110

I Fliegerkorps
Long-range reconnaissance
   5./(F)122   Ju88, He111
Long-range bombers
  KG76 Stab, I, III   Do17
  II./KG76   Ju88
  KG77 Stab, I, II, III   Ju88
  KG1 Stab, I, II   He111
  III./KG1   Ju88
  KG30 Stab, I, II   Ju88

II Fliegerkorps
Long-range reconnaissance
   1./(F)122   Ju88
   7./(F)LG2   Me110
Long-range bombers
  KG2 Stab, I, II, III   Do17z
  KG53 Stab, I, II, III   He111
  KG3 Stab, I, II, III   Do17z
  IV./(St)LG1   Ju87
Fighter-bombers
  II (Schlacht)./LG2   Bf109
  Epr.Gr.210   Bf109, Me110
Dive-bombers
  Stab./St.G1   Ju88, Ju87
  II./St.G1   Ju87

VIII Fliegerkorps
Long-range reconnaissance
   7./(F)LG2   Do17
   2./(F)11   Do17
   2./(F)123   Ju88
Fighter-bombers
  V./(Z)LG1   Me110

Dive-bombers
    Stab./St.G2   Do17, Ju87
    II./St.G2   Ju87
    Stab./St.G77   Do17, Ju87
    St.G77 I, II, III   Ju87

IX Fliegerdivision
Long-range reconnaissance
    3./(F)122   Ju88, He111
    KG4 Stab, I, II   He111
    III./KG4   Ju88
Mine-laying
    KGr.126   He111
    Stab./KG40   Ju88
Coastal reconnaissance
    K.Fl.Gr106   Hc115, Do18

Jagdfliegerführer 1
Fighter
    JG76 Stab, II   Bf109
Fighter-bomber
    V.(Z)./LG1   Me110

Jagdfliegerführer 2
Fighters
    JG53 Stab, I, II, III   Bf109
    Stab./JG51   Bf109
    JG3   Bf109

Luftgaukommando VI
Fighters
    I./JG52 (one Schwarm)   Bf109
    III./JG3 (one Schwarm)   Bf109

Luftgaukommando XI
Fighters
    Stab./JG1   Bf109
    II./JG52   Bf109
    II./JG51   Bf109

Luftgaukommando Holland
Fighters
    JG54 I, II, III (one Schwarm each)   Bf109
    II./JG51 (one Schwarm)   Bf109

Luftgaukommando Belgium
Close reconnaissance aircraft only

LUFTFLOTTE 3

Aufkl.Gr123 Stab
Long-range reconnaissance
    1./(F)123   Ju88, Do17
    2./(F)123   Ju88, Do17
    3./(F)123   Ju88, Do17

Jagdfiegerführer 3

IV Fliegerkorps
Long-range reconnaissance
    3./(F)121   Ju88, He111
    LG1 Stab, I, II, III and reserve Staffel   Ju88
Dive-bombers
    St.G3 Stab, I, II   Ju87
    St.G2   Ju87
Long-range bombers
    K.Gr.806   Ju88
    KG27 Stab, I, II, III and reserve Staffel   He111
    K.Gr.100   He111
    K.Gr.606   Do17
Long-range reconnaissance
    3./(F)31   Me110, Do17
Naval cooperation
    I./KG40   Fw200
Fighters
    ZG76 Stab, II, III   Me110
    JG53 Stab, I,II, III   Bf109
    V./LG1   Me110

V Fliegerkorps
Long-range reconnaissance
    4./(F)121   Ju88, Do17
    4./(F)14   Me110, Do17
Long-range bombers
    KG51 Stab, I, II, III and
      reserve Staffel   Ju88
    KG54 Stab, I, II and reserve
      Staffel   Ju88
    KG55 Stab, I, II, III and reserve Staffel   He111
Fighters
    ZG26 Stab, I, II, III   Me110
    JG2 Stab, I, II, III   Bf109
    JG27 Stab, I, II, III   Bf109

LUFTFLOTTE 5 (Holland)

X Fliegerkorps

Long-range reconnaissance
    Stab./(F)22   Do17
    2./(F)22   Do17
    1./(F)120   Ju88, He111
    1./(F)121   Ju88, Do17
    3./(F)122   Ju88, Do17

Coastal reconnaissance
    Aufkl.Gr.Ob.d.1.Ku.FlGr.506 (one Kette) He115
    1./506   He115
    2./506   He115
    3./506   He115

Fighters
    II./JG77   Bf109

Who Were the Few?
by Tony Mansell

THIS ARTICLE provides one answer to the question Who Were the Few? in terms of how they came to be in the Battle in the first place. Let us begin with the pilots. To have taken part a pilot must have entered the AAF, the RAF or one of its various Direct Entry Reserves prior to the outbreak of the war or, as in a small number of cases, in its opening months. Ten months elapsed between the outbreak of the war and the commencement of the Battle – a short time in which to train a pilot to operational standard – hence the overwhelming majority of pilots who took part were pre-war entrants. Most were British but there were also men from the Empire who had enlisted in the RAF or its reserves, or who came to fight alongside them. Pilots arrived who had served in European air forces, the Belgians, the Czechs, the French and the Poles. Eleven Americans took part, as did nine Irishmen. Not all pilots were initially trained for the fighter role. During the Battle, some Fairey Battle and Lysander pilots volunteered for transfer to Fighter Command. The statistics and comments, which follow, show the contributions of the various portals of entry to the Service and hence to the Battle itself. The data is up-to-date at the time of writing (2006) but, even at this remove, the Battle of Britain Fighter Association still debates the position of some men on its Master List. Any resulting minor adjustments are unlikely to invalidate the picture concerning pilots and aircrew presented here. All errors are my own.

Table 1. Pilot Entry Categories in the Battle of Britain.

Entry Category (Regulars)	No. in Battle	KIA	% KIA
Cranwell (1)	88	24	28
Direct Entry Permanent Commissions (2)	18	4	19
Short Service Commissions (3)	665	142	21
Aircraft Apprentices (4)	116	22	19
Aircraftmen (5)	48	9	19
Direct Entry Airmen Pilots (6)	30	3	10
Total Regulars	**965**	**204**	**21**
Entry Categories (Reserves)			
Auxiliary Air Force (7)	152	28	18
University Air Squadrons (8)	99	23	24
Auxiliary Air Force Ground/Air Crew (9)	30	8	28
Royal Air Force Volunteer Reserve (10)	797	135	17
Total Reserves	**979**	**172**	**18**
Other Categories			
European Air Forces (11)	271	42	16
Dominion Air Forces (12)	66	4	6
Fleet Air Arm (13)	59	9	16
Total Pilots	**2340**	**431**	**18**

Notes on Table 1.

(1) Cranwell was the portal of entry to the RAF, which, via its Cadetships, was intended to produce men holding Permanent Commissions destined for a lifetime in the Service.

(2) Direct Entry Permanent Commissions were awarded to men who could offer some distinctive qualities or qualifications to the Service and did not entail attendance at Cranwell. A scheme was in force to attract university graduates to such commissions.

(3) The majority of RAF officers held Short Service Commissions, which could be extended in suitable cases or indeed converted to Permanent Commissions. They attracted young men who wanted to fly for a few years and then return to civilian life.

(4) Aircraft Apprentices entered the Service at around 16 years of age and became its highest skilled Grade I

tradesmen. After serving in their trades for a number of years they could apply for training as pilots. If successful they flew for a notional five years (although this could be extended) before resuming their original duties. Apprentice schemes were operated at Halton for mechanical trades, at Cranwell for wireless and electrical trades and at Ruislip for clerks. The majority of the men shown here came from Halton (103) but small numbers of those from Cranwell(8) and Ruislip(5) are included in the total. Each year a number of the best Halton or Cranwell apprentices who had completed their course were awarded Cadetships at Cranwell. Eight of the 88 Cranwell graduates who flew in the Battle were former apprentices, 7 of them from Halton and 1 from Cranwell. They appear in the Cranwell category of Table 1. Of the 116 apprentice entry, 29 flew as officers and 87 as sergeants (28 of them were F/Sgts).

(5) Some tradesmen enlisted in the RAF as Boy Entrants or as Aircraftmen and received their training without passing through the Apprentice system. Like their Apprentice colleagues they were eligible for pilot training. Of the 48 Aircraft-hand entry, 7 flew as officers and 41 as Sergeant Pilots (3 were F/Sgts and one WO is included with them).

(6) A scheme to recruit Direct Entry Airmen Pilots (DEAP) operated for a short period in the mid 1930s. The scheme foundered because it was unpopular in the Service, especially with the tradesmen who had hoped to fill the pilot vacancies taken up by such men themselves and who also resented the award of Sergeant rank to the newcomers which it had taken them many years of service to attain. Of the 30 DEAP men, 12 flew as officers and 18 as Sergeant Pilots.

(7) The AAF was similar to the TA and the RNVR in providing a civilian-based force, which could be drawn upon in time of war. It was an extremely élitist organisation, entry to which relied heavily on wealth and social position, consequently it was never up to its established strength. Initially all its pilots were officers but

see also Note 9 below. Originally intended as bomber and
army cooperation units, the majority of AAF squadrons
were converted to the fighter role in the mid-30s. In the
Battle its former squadrons, by then operationally
indistinguishable from those of the RAF, were manned by
men from virtually every category of entry represented in
Table 1.

(8) University Air Squadrons (UAS) were established at
Cambridge and Oxford in 1925 and at London in 1935.
Up to September 1938 members were not under any
obligation to enter either the RAF or any of its Direct
Entry Reserves but many did so voluntarily. Class AA of
the Reserve of Air Force Officers (RAFO) provided a
useful source of income for an undergraduate whilst he
continued with his studies. In the Battle the 99 former
members of the university squadrons had made their way
into the AAF (11), RAFVR (74), Short Service
Commissions (5), Direct Entry Permanent Commissions
(9).

(9) In 1938 the AAF was forced by the Air Ministry to
start training some of its ground or aircrew members as
pilots. It had refused to cooperate in the training of the
RAFVR. Men became Sergeant Pilots but 9 were
commissioned by the time of the Battle.

(10) The RAFVR, which was set up in 1936, became the
major Direct Entry Reserve. It aimed to recruit men from
the widest possible spectrum of society and was referred to
by the Air Ministry as a 'democratic reserve'. Its recruits
were initially enrolled as potential sergeant pilots but
commissions were available for men having the required
attributes, e.g. former UAS and RAFO Class AA men, and
also for those who demonstrated their worth whilst
serving. The RAFO had two classes for pilots. Class A
contained men who had previously served as such in the
RAF. Class AA was composed of men who had not seen
full-time service with the RAF and who may or may not
have had flying experience gained elsewhere. A total of 52
Battle of Britain pilots held RAFO Class AA commissions
at some stage of their flying careers but subsequently

entered the AAF (6), RAFVR (22) or took short service (20) or permanent commissions (4). On the formation of the RAFVR Class AA men were invited to transfer their commissions to those of the RAFVR and this has been allowed for in Table 1. Also included in the 797 RAFVR pilots shown in Table 1 are some who had been in Class F, a Direct Entry Reserve that for a short period pre-dated the RAFVR, and a number of men who volunteered for flying duties after conscription. Of the 797 men, 330 flew as officers and 467 as sergeants, 770 of them were pre-war entrants. All men entering the air force after the outbreak of war did so as members of the RAFVR.

(11) Members of European air forces, e.g. the Polish Air Force, made their way to Britain and flew with RAF squadrons. Some of the Poles and Czechs had RAF squadrons formed specifically for them. Such men were experienced pilots, often rather older than their RAF counterparts, and they made an invaluable contribution to the Battle. The nationalities were as follows, Belgian (24), Czech (88), French (13) and Polish (146).

(12) Australia, Canada, Jamaica, New Zealand, Newfoundland and South Africa/Rhodesia contributed at least 254 pilots, mainly through men who had taken RAF commissions during the 1930s with the majority coming from Canada and New Zealand. However, 66 of them, principally Canadians and New Zealanders, flew with RAF squadrons whilst remaining members of their national air forces. Included in those 66 are the pilots of 1(RCAF) Squadron, which fought alongside its RAF colleagues. There are some difficulties in determining the exact nationality of a few citizens of what we now know as the Commonwealth so I have not attempted to be specific here.

(13) The Fleet Air Arm loaned some of its pilots to the RAF and placed two of its own squadrons, Nos 804 and 808, under Fighter Command control.

We turn now to those who flew in the Battle, not as pilots but as members of the crews of Blenheim and Defiant

squadrons and of the FIU. The Battle of Britain as
experienced by them, and their pilots, was different from
that of the Hurricane and Spitfire men but the contribution
they made was a vital one.

Table 2. Battle of Britain Aircrew Categories.

Category/Rank	Aircraftmen	NCOs	Officers	Total	KIA
Air Gunner	2	226	67	295	31
WOp/Air Gunner		96		96	11
Radar Operator	75	24	2	101	9
Observer		67	35	102	11

Table 3. Modes of Entry of Non-Pilot Aircrew.

Pre-War RAF	AAF	RAFVR	War Entry RAFVR	Total Aircrew
134	55	168	234	594*

*This figure includes three men whose mode of entry is unknown to me.

Notes on Tables 2 and 3.

Aircraftmen ranks are those below Corporal. Most of the
Pre-War Regulars enlisted in such ranks, a few were Boy
Entrants and 11 later became commissioned. The AAF
recruited non-commissioned ground and aircrew as did the
RAFVR. Conscripted men, shown under War Entry, could
volunteer for flying duties. Of the War Entry, 32 were men
who had volunteered in New Zealand, most of whom flew
with the RAF as members of the RNZAF - one of them was
in fact Australian. Four others came from Belgium, 1 from
Ireland and 1 from Canada.

   Hurricane and Spitfire pilots come most readily to mind
when speaking of The Few but 594 non-pilot aircrew flew
under Fighter Command control in the Battle and 62 of
them lost their lives. Their aircraft were no match for the
Luftwaffe's Bf109s, or even the Bf110s. Defiant crews,
who account for 17 of the 31 air gunners killed, were at
great risk once that aircraft had lost its initial element of
surprise. Blenheims flew as escorts for bombing raids on
the French coast, for minelayers and for Channel convoys.
They carried out reconnaissance missions and played a vital

role in the development of Air Interception (AI) Radio Direction Finding (RDF) techniques , which were Fighter Command's only hope of dealing with the coming German night offensive. The effectiveness of some of the Blenheim squadrons was enhanced as the Beaufighter began to enter service with them in late August and early September. The majority of AI operators, some of whom were re-deployed wireless operators(air), flew in Aircraftmen ranks but this does not reflect their quality. In the heat of the Battle with the prospect of a night offensive looming, ground tradesmen serving as wireless operators or wireless mechanics volunteered for service as AI operators and were employed with no regard to rank. The term Radar (Radio Direction and Range) was not formally recognised by the RAF until 1943 but has been used for convenience here in Table 2.

This is an updated version (2006) of my article Who Were the Few that appeared in 2001 in Issue No 1 of 1940 the magazine of Friends of the Few, published by the Battle of Britain Memorial Trust. I am grateful for their permission to reproduce its format here.

No, 43 Squadron
Battle of Britain Roll of Honour

19.07.40	Sgt J A Black	Killed in Action	Hurricane Mk 1	P3531
20.07.40	Flg Off. J F J Haworth	Killed in Action	Hurricane Mk 1	P3946
21.07.40	Plt Off. R A De Mancha	Killed in Action	Hurricane Mk 1	P3973
29.07.40	Plt Off. K C Campbell	Killed in Action	Hurricane Mk 1	L1955
08.08.40	Plt Off. J Cruttenden	Killed in Action	Hurricane Mk 1	P3781
08.08.40	Plt Off. J R S Oelofse	Killed in Action	Hurricane Mk 1	P3468
14.08.40	Sgt H F Montgomery	Killed in Action	Hurricane Mk 1	L1739
30.08.40	Sqd. Ldr J V C Badger, DFC	Died of Wounds	Hurricane Mk 1	V6548
30.08.40	Sgt D Noble	Killed in Action	Hurricane Mk1	P3179
02.09.40	Plt Off. C A Wood-Scawen, DFC	Killed in Action	Hurricane Mk 1	V7420
07.09.40	Sqd. Ldr C B Hull, DFC	Killed in Action	Hurricane Mk 1	V6641
07.09.40	Flt Lt. R C Reynell	Killed in Action	Hurricane Mk 1	V7257
24.10.40	Sgt D R Stoodley	Flying Accident	Hurricane Mk 1	V7303
27.10.40	Sgt L V Toogood	Killed in Action	Hurricane Mk 1	L1963

Lt Cdr W B Luard, RN

Lieutenant Commander W B Luard first joined DDOD(I) as an unpaid volunteer in the autumn of 1940, and played a leading part in the early investigations into fishing vessel operations to the north coast, as opposed to the Biscay coast, of France.

In January 1942, when the enemy had prohibited all offshore fishing activities from ports on the north coast, Lt Cdr Luard was appointed to the RAF Station St Eval, as DDOD(I)'s naval operations liaison officer.

Thereafter, for over 2 years, he rendered outstanding service in arranging for the provision of intelligence, including special sorties to obtain information on French fishing vessel movements in the Bay of Biscay: air escort on the outward and homeward daylight passages of the Inshore Patrol Flotilla through no man's land, and for the 15th MGB Flotilla: search and patrol for overdue ships, etc. These duties included many hours spent in operational flying combat areas and, in the early days, Luard himself conducted the navigation of the search and patrol aircraft.

In 1943, the Admiralty entrusted him with the organisation of two large-scale combined air/surface sweeps for rounding up French tunny vessels in the western approaches to the Bay of Biscay, whose presence was a hindrance to the RAF anti-submarine campaign.

Side by side with these activities, Luard, who was an expert in small craft design and performance, rendered invaluable service in the design and production of the following equipment:

K-dinghy sailing gear.
Aircraft catamaran dinghy.   Air/sea rescue
RAF dinghy drift tables.

Submarine target for training
crews in anti-submarine work.   RAF Coastal Command
Handbook of fishing industries.

Design of catamaran power-driven
canoes for irregular operations
by submarine and unorthodox   DDOD(I) and CCO
offensive warfare in the Eastern Theatre.

Having in 1943 been awarded the *Croix de Guerre* with Lt Cdr Mackenzie and Lt Cdr Whinney, for his contribution to irregular operations on behalf of France, he was in 1944 officially thanked by the Air Council for the work described above.

Lt Cdr Luard was originally invalided from submarine service in World War I with a tubercular hip, and this left him badly lame. In spite of this disability he served in a fully operational appointment with DDOD(I) for over four years – being more active than many people who were not handicapped.

With the reduction of irregular operations in Home Waters, his duties came to an end and he shortly left DDOD(I) to pursue other spheres of activity.

After World War II Lt Cdr Luard became a very successful writer. Apart from books covering the technical aspects of seafaring he also wrote many novels about the sea including 'All Hands', 'Wild Goose Chase' and 'Conquering Seas', which received many favourable reviews.

Archaeology Reports of a Me 110 shot down by TDM

The History of a Luftwaffe Aircraft shot down in the Battle of Britain.

Messerschmitt Me110C-1, Code 2N+DP, Werke Nr 2837
Unit: Stab III./ZG76
Crew: Oblt **Helmut Florenz (Pilot & Staffelführer),**
Gefr **Rudi Hebert** (Bordfunker).
Shot down by Flt Lieut Tom Dalton-Morgan of 43 Squadron.
Crashed and exploded at Church Farm, Washington, Pulborough, Sussex on the 4th September 1940.

This particular aircraft and its mission encapsulates many facets of the Battle of Britain that have captivated the public for over sixty years.

On this day the *Luftwaffe* performed one of the most successful low level attacks during the Battle. It was carried out by fourteen *Zerstörer* (Destroyer) aircraft of *Erprobungsgruppe 210* on the Vickers Armstrong works at Weybridge in Surrey where they accurately dropped six 500kg bombs on the assembly sheds and machine shops. This *Gruppe* was trained and primed with the specific purpose of attacking this type of target and only lost one aircraft in the raid.

However, the escorting fighters of Me110s were not so lucky and suffered grievous losses when sixteen aircraft were shot down over the Weybridge plant and the South Downs. The total *Luftwaffe* losses for the day amounted to twenty-eight aircraft of which seventeen were Me110s.

Losses at this level were unsustainable for the Me110 and this raid, together with further disastrous raids, instigated the change in role for the heavy day fighter to that of a night fighter. This, at the time, represented a significant victory for the RAF.

After the Second World War the interest in the Battle of Britain continued and this led to the start and growth of aviation archaeology. Various groups researched the available records and began 'digging up' German and British aircraft shot down during the Battle. One of the first of these groups included two pioneers of aircraft archaeology, Peter Foote and Dennis Knight, who were responsible for the 'dig' on this aircraft. Their respective record of this event follows together with a subsequent report by Phillipa Hodgkiss.

Her record is a tribute to the early ground breaking efforts of both Peter Foote and Dennis Knight and highlights the painstaking and meticulous research involved.

A fuel tank mounting bracket, which survived the crash, was mounted on a wooden plaque and given to 43 Squadron at Leuchars in 2000. It is called the 'Air Weapons Excellence' Trophy and the first recipient of the trophy, was presented with it by Bill Littlemore in 2000.

It is a fitting link that recognizes the contribution made by 43 Squadron during the Battle of Britain and the current Squadron now flying Tornados from RAF Leuchars in Scotland.

Report by Peter Foote

Wed. 4th September. 1940.

Me110 down at Washington, burnt out. No trace of crew, believed dead.

Me110 crashed near Washington churchyard at 13.30 hrs. A/C dived into a field from great height in flames and wreckage now lies buried as flames were lighting up the position of No, 461 Battery RA during the raid.
Crater found by the crash about 20 ft deep and the A/C was completely destroyed.
Crew of 2 reported to be buried in the wreckage.

14.05 hrs   Me110 crashed in flames at CHURCH FM Washington. Crew killed and buried. A/C burst into flame.
local eye witness told me it was not on fire as it nose dived down.

A supplement stated:- The wreckage of another Me110 found at WASHINGTON, near Pulborough. Owing to its condition, no identification of any kind was possible. According to local reports, the crash occurred at the same time as that of the one NW of Pulborough, i.e., 13.30 hrs.

1.30PM
Bf110C-1   WN 2837   2N+DP of StabIII/ZG76 shot down by Flt Lt. T F DALTON-MORGAN of 43 Sq during fighter combat over SHOREHAM possibly also attacked by Sgt M C B BODDINGTON 234 Sq. Crashed and exploded at CHURCH FARM, WASHINGTON Nr PULBOROUGH.
Oberlt. H FLORENZ and Gefr. R HERBERT of 8/ZG76 both missing believed killed.
This A/C dived straight into the ground and exploded with such violence that no trace of the crew was ever reported found.
The site, now under a new road, was excavated in 1965 by a group of enthusiasts including:-   Christopher Elliott
                                               Peter Foote
                                               Dennis Knight

Both DB601 engines, propellers, u/c, many components and manufacturer's labels were unearthed together with partial remains of the crew.
During later road development work construction workers uncovered a complete parachute pack now in Peter Foote collection.

A Saunders sent me obituary on Intelligence Officer John Peskett who died 7/3/91.   Andy recalled whilst having borrowed his war time note book Peskett had visited the crash and recorded the WN.

August 1996. Graham Lewis of Crediton and Freddie Walford of SW Aviation Historical Society visited having requested to see Bf109, WN 1190, before I disposed of it.
Whilst letting them have a selection of bits out of a dust bin full of 110 items from NORTH BADDESLEY, Freddie Walford spotted a DB601 engine valve with portion of Cyl. head still attached.   It had a label identifying as WASHINGTON. I compared the details, date of crash, when dug, and my name. He asked could he have it, as they don't have any such 110s in West Country.

Take call Brian HUTTON 19/11/97
He has been back to site on edge of road and been to see scrap merchant - an engine has gone on display somewhere, they have an u/c leg.

Report by Dennis Knight
Report: crash site Washington, W. Sussex

INTRODUCTION

Police report in Chichester message log: At 1405 hours, 4th September, 1940, an Me110 crashed in flames at Church Farm, Washington.

This machine was one of several Me110s that were engaged by Hurricanes of No. 1 (RCAF) Sqdn, No. 43 Sqdn (Tangmere) and No. 253 Sqdn (Kenley), over Surrey and Sussex. The Me110s belonged to ZG26 'Horst wessel' and ZG1 'Wespen' Geschwaders, and were escorting bombers that had attacked the Vickers Works at Weybridge.

The main action took place over E Grinstead and was a running battle back to the coast, eight were shot down.

The machine that fell at Washington was seen to fly over from the NW at some 6,000 feet chased by a Hurricane. Several bursts of gunfire rang out over the Downs and the Messerschmitt burst into flames and nosed down striking the ground at high speed and exploding.

All that was left was a blazing crater in a field just west of Church Farm. The setting is delightful, a little dale nestling in a fell in the Downs with the ancient church only 200 yds away. Chanctonbury Ring dominates the scene from above and only a mile to the NE id the Windmill in which Vaughn Williams lived.

SURVEY

I reached the site at 10.00 hours, 28th Feb. 65, and visited the local farmer Mr Turner gaining permission to survey the site, which was easily recognisable being a shallow depression in the field as seen on my previous visit in 1963.

MR. 117127 Sheet 182

Dr Hall with two operators arrived in the village with the Prot-Magnetometer from Oxford at 10.20 hours. Mr Peter Foote of Bournemouth arrived at 10.30 hours and we commenced staking out the dig.

Dr Hall took several sets of readings in a 1 foot grid and we came to the opinion that a considerable amount of ferrous metal was under the ground at a depth of about 6 feet.

We adjourned for lunch at a nearby Inn at 12.30 hours and made a study of the readings. Dr Hall was of the opinion that we would certainly find something fairly large under the ground, ie., an engine or similar, in the northern corner of the crater. Dr Hall left after lunch and Mr Foote and myself decided to put down a pilot excavation hole. Prior to doing this I visited Miss Beecher to ask her permission since the land is still owned by her and her family. Miss Beecher lives in a converted stable that once belonged to Rowdell House which was demolished just after the war. Rowdell House, a very substantial mansion, overlooked the scene at the time and it was the Beecher's butler who first reached the blazing wreck. (The Beecher family gave their name to the famous Grand National obstacle.)

PILOT EXCAVATION

Digging over the spot which registered the maximum instrument reading, we found several German 7.69 mm cartridge cases and bullets at the same depth of approximately 2 feet. Some of these were still held together with the hinged iron links.

Most had burst open having exploded in the heat of the fire. Below these were sundry fragments of aircraft, mostly aluminium and badly corroded. More bullets were found and in all some 30 cartridge cases. It was most interesting to note that several cartridges had been fired – the machine gun striker-pin marks being visible on the percussion caps.

At approx. 3 feet 6" heavy clods of earth baked to brick hardness were found and bore evidence to the extreme heat of the blaze.

At 4 feet 6" a heavy piece of light alloy frame was uncovered. This ran down into the ground and a similar structure projected off at an angle deeper into the ground. An iron wing spar strap of the type fitted to an Me110 was uncovered and this appears to go very deep into the earth and to be attached to the alloy structure.

Having satisfied myself that there were identifiable portions of the machine still under the ground – possibly one or more engines and or the main armament – we filled in the pilot hole with straw bales and cleared up the site.

Before leaving the area I visited the plant hire depot of Hall & Co. Ltd on the Storrington Road. Mr Rusbridge proved most helpful and agreed to furnish me with a JCB digger at £1.10.3d per hour if required.

CONCLUSIONS & RECOMMENDATIONS

I feel that the site will yield some heavy structure from an Me110 which should prove photographic, coupled with this a considerable amount of ammunition will be found I believe. Beyond this, I can only conjecture at that which could be unearthed.

I feel there is little likelihood of finding anything of the crew which is probably for the best. The crew members perished in the crash and there is some suggestion that the few remains that were found were put back into the crater since the Washington inhabitants refused to have them buried in the local churchyard.

The crew identity discs were fire proof and although it is unlikely we could find them it may be possible to identify the crew if a *Werk Nr.* plate can be found on the structure.

If you should instruct me to proceed with the projected excavation at the site, I intend to have a 6 feet deep, 6 feet wide, trench dug some 10 feet away from the crater running N to S so as to take off successive layers of earth, searching as the stratis progressively go deeper.

The whole task should be completed in 3 days assuming that we do not have inclement weather.

Mr Turner and his family should prove most cooperative and I have told them that there would no publicity during any excavation so as to avoid crowds and sightseers.

Incidentally a new duel carriage way, crossing the Downs, is scheduled to run straight through the site! And work is expected to commence shortly.

A Pioneer Dig – Sussex 1965
A Look Back by Phillipa Hodgkiss

It is perhaps inevitable with the near exhaustion of sites in the South East of England from the Battle of Britain period that the veterans of the frantic digging days of the 1970s and early 80s should look nostalgically back to those times.

Some years ago I was driving down the A24 towards Worthing with the late Peter Foote when we turned off for Shoreham-on-Sea at Washington. A new road swept below the South Downs and, as we sped by, Peter pointed out an area where he had buried what remained of the crew of an Me110 at a field edge, We had, he said, just driven over the impact crater. He had been one of the first to do a 'dig', something that clearly gave some satisfaction. He and a few others who had witnessed the Battle of Britain rage overhead had kept their boyhood interest, had searched scanty official records, books and local memory for elusive detail, visited country churchyards and recorded findings in painful longhand illustrated with yellowing photographs. As a colleague with a fondness for aphorisms remarked, 'the worst ink survives the best memory'. So it does and so it was I found the story of the Washington 110 in the 'Foote Notes'.

A year and a day after the outbreak of war the Observer Corps at Guilford reported about twenty Me110s flying north at about 6,000 feet, shortly afterwards these arrived over the unmistakable concrete oval of Brooklands' track and carried out a short, but damaging, raid on the Vickers Works which left 700 casualties and 87 dead. In doing so six of their number from ZG76 remained behind south of Weybridge where they had fallen to the guns of 253 Squadron. As the survivors fled south towards the Channel their *Gruppen kameraden* of III,/ZG76 were racing eastwards along the Channel coast to form a defensive circle north of Worthing where they were attacked by Spitfires and the Hurricanes of 43 Squadron. Even hindsight and analysis leaves loose ends in sorting out the melee which followed and to those on the ground it must have been even more confusing.

Eyewitnesses saw an Me110, pursued by a Hurricane, nose over into a dive which steepened to the vertical as it howled to earth, a dive which ended abruptly at Church Farm, Washington, when it disappeared entirely into a crater of its own making. It was some time before sightseers and prospective souvenir hunters could approach the spot as ammunition cooked off in the fire which smouldered on and off for a fortnight, the farmer remarking he could see nothing in the hole but twisted fragments. Intelligence Officer, F/O Peskett, noted the *werk nummer* in his report but there was little else to report on so the hole was filled-in leaving a small depression in the field. It would be a further twenty-five years before the remains of Nr. 2837 would again see the light of day. There must have been many glum faces and empty seats in the messes at Laval on the evening of 4th September, 1940.

The victory has been variously attributed to S/Ldr Caesar Hull, CO of 43, and to F/Lt Tom Dalton Morgan who was to succeed Hull as CO when he was killed over Purley three days later.

On an overcast day late in October 1963 the celebrated aviation historian Dennis Knight with Peter Foote met former policeman George Clout at the site. There was the depression still to be seen in the field. In February 1965 the two researchers were joined by a Dr Hall of Oxford who ran a proton-magnetometer over the crater and gave as his opinion that the readings showed significant buried remains. They began an exploratory dig. Ammunition, some exploded by heat and others showing the striker marks of being fired in action were discovered two feet down. At three feet the clay was baked brick hard by heat. At four feet substantial pieces of airframe were encountered, too deeply embedded to be dislodged. Satisfied that a recovery could be attempted the hole was backfilled. Local enquiries established a mechanical digger could be hired for £1.10.3d per hour.

Later in the year, in mid June, the two men were joined by another well known historian, Chris Elliott, and Peter's lifelong friend, the late Gordon Bailey, was also a visitor.

Both a Massey Ferguson excavator and a tractor with lifting jib and chains were used to extract wreckage over several days. Oddly, the Foote Notes, so often detailing the minutiae of recovered items, are largely silent on what was found, though photographs show a farm trailer loaded with debris. It is believed both engines with undercarriages also came to light and that at least one of the engines survives. The photographs show a buckled *Luftwaffe* NCO's belt buckle and a British 1939 half-crown bent and discoloured by heat – possible souvenir of a Channel Islands visit. These, together with a gas mask and its case, and some scant human remains, were apparently all that was found of the crew. Interestingly the gas mask contained a diary and, over the years, there has been some speculation as to its content. When helping to clear Peter's home after his death last year a box of relics from the Washington aircraft came to light in the attic. There indeed was the diary, if diary it was, charred beyond recognition or any reading. Of such are legends made. Apparently much of the aircraft went for scrap as have so many relics of the Battle. Not quite all, because the file contains some correspondence which suggests a piece of the aircraft forms part of a trophy – 'The Battle of Britain Fighting Cocks Trophy' – awarded annually to the person 'most contributing to the air fighting potential of No, 43(F) Squadron'. So the aircrew of today are linked to their gallant predecessors of sixty years ago. It is remarkable that this pioneer dig, undertaken nearly four decades ago, has all the elements of a 'modern dig' in its use of deep seeking equipment and mechanical plant. As the new road was driven through in the face of local opposition it crossed the site and a parachute was found and passed into the Foote Collection.

If you pass through Washington, spare a thought for the two young men who never went home and who may lie beneath your speeding wheels.

Bf110c-1   Nr. 2837   2N+DP   III./ZG76
Oblt. H Florenz (pilot)   Gefr. R Herbert   8./ZG76

APPENDIX 8

Details of Aircraft
Flown by TDM
(Prepared by Geoffrey Dalton Morgan)

1	Avro 504K	25	Hawker Typhoon
2	Link Trainer	26	Miles Martinet
3	de Havilland Gipsy Moth	27	Airspeed Oxford
4	Hawker Hart Trainer	28	General Aircraft Monospar
5	Hawker Audex	29	Percival Proctor
6	Fairey II F	30	Miles Monarch
7	Fairey Seal	31	Westland Whirlwind
8	Vickers Vildebeest	32	de Havilland Dominie
9	Fairey Swordfish	33	Gloster Meteor
10	Avro Tutor	34	Douglas Dakota
11	Miles Magister	35	Taylorcraft Auster
12	Avro Anson	36	Hawker Tempest
13	Percival Vega Gulf	37	Miles Messenger
14	Miles Mentor	38	de Havilland Mosquito
15	Hawker Osprey	39	Fieseler Storch
16	North American Harvard	40	Avro York
17	Hawker Hurricane	41	de Havilland Vampire
18	Gloster Gladiator	42	Vickers Viking
19	Miles Master	43	de Havilland DH-148 Dove
20	de Havilland Tiger Moth	44	de Havilland Venom
21	Supermarine Spitfire II	45	de Havilland DHC3 Otter
22	Supermarine Seafire	46	Sud-Aviation Alouette
23	North American Mustang	47	English Electric Canberra
24	de Havilland DH-87B Hornet Moth	48	Beechcraft Kingair

1 Avro 504K

First Flight	Last Flight	Hours
10-Nov-34	4-Dec-34	6:45

Description	2 seat *ab initio* trainer
Dimensions	Span 36ft Length 29ft 5in
Performance	Max speed 95mph Range 250 miles

2 Link Trainer

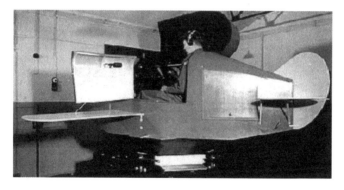

First Flight	Last Flight	Hours
10-Jul-39	27-Nov-42	12:35

The **RAF Link Trainer** was used to instruct pilots inblind flying. It has a small cabin, large enough for one person to sit in, that is used to simulate blind flying, a situation in which the weather conditions prevent the pilot from being able to see clearly.

3 De Havilland Gipsy Moth

Number	Ist Flight	Last Flight	Hours	
T A	27-Aug-35	17-Oct-35	48:45	Bristol Flying School
B C	14-Oct-35	14-Oct-35	0:35	
I W	15-Oct-35	17-Oct-35	1:50	
Z Y	17-Oct-35	17-Oct-35	0:45	
G.ABRO	10-Feb-37	19-Mar-38	1:50	'A' Flight, 22 (B) Sqd
G.ABJG	11-Aug-37	11-Aug-38	1:10	

Description	2 seat trainer and communications
Dimensions	Span 30ft Length 23ft 11in
Performance	Max speed 105mph Range 280-320mls

4 Hawker Hart Trainer

K4963	4-Nov-35	25-Nov-35	9:20	No.11 Flying TS
K495	18-Nov-35	14-Jan-36	2:35	
K4960	26-Nov-35	20-Jan-36	1:00	
K4961	26-Nov-35	17-Jan-36	3:50	
K4967	29-Nov-35	29-Nov-35	0:25	
K4966	29-Nov-35	20-Jan-36	2:00	
K4979	2-Dec-35	23-Dec-35	2:45	
K4969	9-Jan-36	20-Jan-36	4:10	
K4982	24-Feb-36	23-Apr-36	4:20	

Description	2 seat advanced trainer
Dimensions	Span 37ft 4in Length 29ft 4in
Performance	Max speed 165mph Range 430 miles

5   Hawker Audax

Number	Ist Flight	Last Flight	Hours	
K4405	25-Nov-35	6-Jan-36	9:10	No.11 FTS
K4398	2-Dec-35	6-Jan-36	1:50	
K4406	9-Dec-35	20-Jan-36	5:35	
K5213	18-Feb-36	27-Apr-36	29:00	
K5127	6-Mar-36	6-Mar-36	1:30	
K5132	16-Mar-36	27-Apr-36	1:15	
K5211	19-Mar-36	31-Mar-36	1:25	
K5210	29-Apr-36	29-Apr-36	1:35	
K5128	30-Apr-36	30-Apr-36	0:45	

Description	2 seat advanced trainer
Dimensions	Span 37ft 3in Length 29ft 7in
Performance	Max speed 170mph Endurance 3 1/2hrs

6   Fairey III F

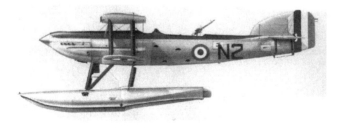

S1851	22-Jun-36	22-Jun-36	0:30	TS Gosport

Description	2 seat general purpose
Dimensions	Span 45ft 9in Length 36ft 9in
Performance	Max speed 120mph Range 400 miles
Armament	1xVickers 1xLewis Bomb-load 500lb

7   Fairey Seal

Number	Ist Flight	Last Flight	Hours	
K3535	24-Jun-36	24-Jun-36	0:30	TS Gosport
K4791	24-Jun-36	24-Jun-36	0:35	

Description	3 seat Bomber and general purpose
Dimensions	Span 45ft 9in Length 36ft 9in
Performance	Max speed 145mph Range 600 miles
Armament	1xVickers 1xLewis Bomb-load 500lb

8   Vickers Vildebeest Mark III

K2817	25-Jun-36	11-Jul-36	3:45	TS Gosport
K2812	26-Jun-36	14-Jul-36	0:35	
S1709	10-Jul-36	7-Aug-36	2:50	
K4157	27-Jul-36	5-Aug-36	1:30	
K4604	2-Nov-36	1-Oct-37	27:50	'A' Flight, 22 (B) Sqd
K4614	4-Nov-36	22-Dec-36	6:45	
K4606	20-Nov-36	28-May-37	6:25	
K4613	30-Nov-36	12-Oct-37	45:50	
K4602	22-Dec-36	29-Jun-37	7:35	
K4592	7-Jan-37	27-Oct-38	21:55	
K4610	2-Feb-37	13-Jul-38	211:30	
K4588	15-Feb-37	4-Jul-37	5:45	

Description	3 seat Torpedo bomber
Dimensions	Span 49ft Length 36ft 8in
Performance	Max speed 143mph Range 630 miles
Armament	1xVickers 1xLewis 1x18in torp or 1,000lb bombs

Number	Ist Flight	Last Flight	Hours
K4607	18-Feb-37	10-Mar-37	2:25
K4612	26-Feb-37	15-Jun-38	13:50
K4591	2-Mar-37	14-Apr-39	11:50
K4594	8-Mar-37	8-May-37	1:20

Vickers Vildebeest Mark IV

K6413	26-Aug-37	26-Aug-37	0:40	Mk IV
K4693	29-Sep-37	29-Sep-37	3:00	
K4598	30-Sep-37	12-Apr-39	13:35	
K4603	1-Oct-37	30-Aug-38	12:15	
K4593	8-Oct-37	21-Mar-38	13:45	
K4605	11-Oct-37	1-Oct-38	2:25	
K4692	6-Dec-37	6-Dec-37	0:30	
K4589	17-Feb-38	5-Nov-38	6:50	
K4197	4-Apr-38	4-Apr-38	1:00	
K6395	13-Apr-38	14-Dec-38	11:45	
K4187	11-Jun-38	15-Jun-38	1:35	
K4609	16-Jun-38	16-Jun-38	1:00	Mk IV
K6397	12-Jul-38	31-Aug-38	10:15	
K4597	2-Sep-38	11-Apr-39	9:45	
K6396	26-Sep-38	13-May-39	97:45	
K4596	17-Oct-38	28-Mar-39	5:05	
K6401	13-Dec-38	13-Dec-38	0:30	
K4595	20-Feb-39	1-May-39	2:00	

Description	2 seat Torpedo bomber
Dimensions	Span 49ft Length 37ft 8in
Performance	Max speed 156mph Range 630miles
Armament	1xVickers 1xLewis 1x18in torp or 1,000lb bombs

9   Fairey Swordfish

Number	Ist Flight	Last Flight	Hours	
K5983	7-Aug-36	7-Aug-36	0:15	Training Squadron Gosport
K5966	10-Aug-36	27-Aug-36	2:30	
K5964	11-Aug-36	16-Sep-36	1:50	
K5962	13-Aug-36	24-Sep-36	0:50	
K5927	14-Aug-36	9-Sep-36	2:25	
K5963	20-Aug-36	9-Sep-36	2:35	
K5965	26-Aug-36	10-Sep-36	1:10	
K5956	26-Aug-36	26-Aug-36	0:40	
K5969	27-Aug-36	27-Aug-36	0:50	

Description	3 seat Reconnaissence, 2 seat Torpedo bomber
Dimensions	Span 45ft 6in Length 36ft 4in
Performance	Max speed 139mph Range 1000miles R, 550 T
Armament	1 Forward 1 Aft .303 1 18in torpedo

10   Avro Tutor

K3339	20-Jul-37	27-Jul-37	4:30	Training Squadron Gosport
K6117	21-Jul-37	29-Jul-37	13:15	
K6115	27-Jul-37	28-Jul-37	1:25	
K3221	30-Jul-37	30-Jul-37	0:50	

Description	2 seat trainer
Dimensions	Span 34ft Length 26ft 6in
Performance	Max speed 122mph Endurance 2 3/4hrs

11   Miles Magister

Number	Ist Flight	Last Flight	Hours	
K6137	14-Aug-38	14-Aug-38	3:00	No.22 (B) Squadron
L8187	16-Sep-38	16-Sep-38	3:00	
N4494	18-May-40	18-May-40	2:15	
L8212	25-May-40	13-Nov-40	4:30	
V1026	11-Feb-41	28-Feb-41	2:05	No.43 Fighter Squadron
P2963	20-Apr-41	30-Apr-41	1:40	
V1101	6-May-41	9-Aug-41	2:35	
R6402	17-Mar-42	17-Mar-42	0:40	
K1105	11-Jul-42	11-Jul-42	0:45	
L8231	24-Oct-42	14-Nov-42	1:50	

Description	2 seat trainer
Dimensions	Span 33ft 10in Length 24ft 8in
Performance	Max speed 132mph Range 367miles

12   Avro Anson

K6661	1-Sep-38	10-Sep-38	5:55	No.22 (B) Squadron
K6311	2-May-39	2-May-39	0:45	
K6310	2-May-39	3-May-39	1:25	
K8714	3-May-39	3-May-39	1:20	
	1-Sep-44	27-Feb-45	9:00	
602	16-Feb-48	16-May-47	45:40	
625	14-Mar-50	20-Jul-50	22:55	
223	23-May-50	23-May-50	0:30	
328	24-Oct-50	10-Feb-51	23:25	
231	29-Jan-51	19-Aug-51	12:40	

Description	3 crew general reconnaissance and transport
Dimensions	Span 56ft 6in Length 42ft 3in
Performance	Max speed 188mph Range 660 miles
Armament	1 Forward 1 turrent .303 bomb-load 360lb

13 Percival Vega Gull

Number	Ist Flight	Last Flight	Hours	
P9551	23-May-39	23-May-39	2:00	No.22 (B) Sqd
G.AFEH	27-Mar-42	4-Sep-42	37:45	No.43 Fighter Sqd

Description	4 seat communications
Dimensions	Span 39ft 6in Length 25ft 6in
Perfomance	Max speed 174mph Range 660 miles

14 Miles Mentor

L4399	5-Jun-39	5-Jun-39	2:10
L4339	17-Aug-39	17-Aug-39	2:40

Description	3 seat radio/navigation trainer
Dimensions	Span 34ft 9in Length 26ft2in
Performance	Max speed 156mph

15 Hawker Osprey

K4297	6-Jun-39	6-Jun-39	1:40

Description	2 seat advanced trainer
Dimensions	Span 37ft Length 29ft 4in
Performance	Max speed 168mph Range 430 miles

16   North American Harvard

Number	Ist Flight	Last Flight	Hours	
N7178	5-Jun-40	5-Jun-40	0:20	6 OTU Sutton Bridge

Description	2 seat advanced trainer
Dimensions	Span 42ft Length 29ft
Performance	Max speed 205mph Range 750miles

17   Hawker Hurricane Mk I

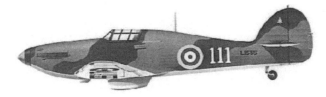

L1924	7-Jun-40	8-Jun-40	2:40	6 OTU Sutton Bridge
N2591	7-Jun-40	9-Jun-40	1:45	
N2469	8-Jun-40	8-Jun-45	1:45	
N2516	10-Jun-40	10-Jun-40	1:45	
N2091	11-Jun-40	11-Jun-40	2:20	
N2534	12-Jun-40	12-Jun-40	1:00	
N2354	12-Jun-40	12-Jun-40	0:40	
L2064	13-Jun-40	13-Jun-40	3:10	
L2070	14-Jun-40	14-Jun-40	1:15	
P3035	14-Jun-40	14-Jun-40	3:05	
L2091	14-Jun-40	14-Jun-40	1:25	
L2057	15-Jun-40	15-Jun-40	0:50	
J3784	18-Jun-40	12-Jul-40	36:15	No.43 Fighter Squadron
K1955	24-Jun-40	16-Jul-05	1:45	
J3466	24-Jun-40	25-Jun-40	2:10	
K1727	28-Jun-40	28-Jun-40	1:15	

Description	1 seat fighter
Dimensions	Span 40ft Length 31ft 5in
Performance	Max speed 316mph Range 460 miles
Armament	8 .303 guns

P3386   Flown by TDM   5-July-1940 + 15-Sept-1940

Number	Ist Flight	Last Flight	Hours	
P3386	5-Jul-40	15-Sep-05	1:30	
P3531	7-Jul-40	7-Jul-40	2:35	
P1739	8-Jul-40	22-Jul-40	1:25	
P3971	12-Jul-40	12-Jul-40	0:20	
P3973	13-Jul-40	13-Jul-40	1:45	
P3964	13-Jul-40	13-Jul-40	0:10	
P3972	13-Jul-40	12-Aug-40	23:30	
P3786	19-Jul-40	19-Jul-40	0:40	
P3216	28-Jul-40	12-Aug-40	13:10	
L1742	4-Aug-40	5-Aug-40	0:40	
P3179	12-Aug-40	12-Aug-40	0:15	
V7542	2-Sep-40	15-Sep-40	5:25	
P2682	5-Sep-40	5-Sep-40	1:15	
V6542	5-Sep-40	14-Sep-40	3:00	
R4231	15-Sep-40	13-Jun-41	120:55	
L1963	6-Oct-40	6-Oct-40	0:55	
V6925	29-Oct-40	29-Oct-40	0:25	
P3466	1-Nov-40	3-Mar-41	1:20	
P2826	5-Nov-40	26-Feb-41	1:15	
V7366	28-Nov-40	28-Nov-40	0:10	
V7206	28-Nov-40	30-Nov-40	1:20	
P2805	24-Nov-40	24-Nov-40	0:25	
V7126	31-Dec-40	16-Jan-41	4:05	
R6231	16-Jan-41	16-Jan-41	1:10	
P3757	23-Jan-41	23-Jan-41	0:15	
P3142	26-Jan-41	26-Jan-41	0:10	
V2436	3-Mar-41	6-Mar-41	0:15	
W9119	5-Mar-41	7-Apr-41	1:30	
V7597	10-Mar-41	10-Mar-41	0:10	
L1983	17-Mar-41	17-Mar-41	0:10	
P2565	17-Mar-41	17-Mar-41	0:10	Mk II
V6537	17-Mar-41	17-Mar-41	0:40	Mk II

Number	Ist Flight	Last Flight	Hours	
Z3149	19-Apr-41	19-Apr-41	0:15	
Z3150	19-Apr-41	16-Jun-41	26:40	Mk II
G4231	19-Apr-41	22-Apr-41	1:25	Mk II
Z2772	24-Apr-41	19-Jul-41	1:05	Mk II
Z2407	4-May-41	4-May-41	0:10	Mk II
Z3265	11-May-41	26-Dec-41	108:25	Mk II
Z3629	12-May-41	12-May-41	0:10	Mk II
Z2388	13-May-41	16-Jun-41	1:40	Mk II
Z3336	17-Jun-41	17-Jun-41	2:10	Mk II
Z3270	18-Jun-41	18-Jun-41	0:15	Mk II
Z3143	21-Jul-41	26-Jul-41	0:55	Mk II
Z3310	2-Oct-41	2-Oct-41	0:40	Mk II
Z2667	27-Oct-41	27-Oct-41	0:10	Mk II
Z3578	18-Nov-41	18-Nov-41	0:10	Mk II
Z2639	21-Nov-41	21-Nov-41	0:30	Mk II
Z2447	23-Nov-41	23-Nov-41	0:10	Mk II
Z2582	23-Nov-41	23-Nov-41	0:10	
Z2775	5-Dec-41	5-Dec-41	0:10	
Z2826	12-Mar-42	12-Mar-42	0:30	Mk XII
P3961	19-Oct-42	2-Feb-43	1:25	
P3981	3-Feb-43	3-Feb-43	0:25	
JS369	30-Aug-45	30-Aug-45	0:15	

18 Gloster Gladiator

K8027	15-Jun-40	15-Jun-40	0:50	No.6 O.T.U. Sutton Bridge

Description	1 seat fighter
Dimensions	Span 32ft 3in Length 27ft 5in
Performance	Max speed 253mph Endurance 2hrs
Armament	4 Browning guns

19   Miles Master

Number	Ist Flight	Last Flight	Hours	
N7654	27-Jul-40	31-Jul-05	1:30	
N7680	25-Dec-40	25-Dec-40	0:35	
M8751	1-Apr-42	1-Apr-42	0:40	
W2362	15-Oct-42	15-Oct-42	1:00	III
T8613	18-Dec-42	21-Mar-43	2:05	
DL529	17-Feb-43	17-Feb-43	1.30	

Description	2 seat advanced trainer
Dimensions	Span 39ft Length 30ft 5in
Performance	Max speed 226mph Range 484 miles

20   de Havilland Tiger Moth

N6930	20-Dec-40	20-Dec-40	0:40	
P2600	21-Apr-41	21-Apr-41		0:55
T1041	4-Apr-42	4-Apr-42	2:20	
K2394	14-Jul-42	15-Jul-42	1:40	
EM428	21-Feb-43	21-Feb-43	0:10	
DX426	25-May-43	25-May-43	0:40	

Description	2 seat elementary trainer
Dimensions	Span 29ft 4in Length 23ft 11in
Performance	Max speed 109mph Range 300 miles

21   Supermarine Spitfire II

Number	Ist Flight	Last Flight	Hours	
P3238	12-Jun-41	12-Jun-41	0:30	
P3438	17-Jul-41	17-Jul-41	0:30	
Z7389	22-Jul-41	22-Jul-41	0:30	
R7308	23-Mar-42	6-Apr-42	1:55	
R6887	13-Apr-42	13-Apr-42	0:45	
W3113	14-Apr-42	25-Apr-42	1:45	
P7352	25-Apr-42	25-Apr-42	0:15	
P7692	25-Apr-42	15-May-42	0:30	
BM423	2-May-42	6-Jun-42	5:00	VB Merlin46
AA424	26-Jun-42	26-Jun-42	0:30 II	
AA739	29-Jun-42	29-Jun-42	1:00 VB	
AA916	5-Jul-42	9-Jul-42	3:15 VB	
AK505	9-Jul-42	9-Jul-42	0:45 IX	
AB405	11-Jul-42	11-Jul-42	1:00	
P7384	13-Jul-42	13-Jul-42	0:15	
AD916	25-Aug-42	25-Aug-42	0:45	
VZM	17-Sep-42	21-Sep-42	2:35	
VZO	17-Sep-42	21-Sep-42	5:45	
VZW	18-Sep-42	18-Sep-42	1:00	
YQL	25-Sep-42	25-Sep-42	2:20 VI	
YQD	26-Sep-42	27-Sep-42	1:50	
VDV	6-Oct-42	6-Oct-42	0:30	
BR160	8-Oct-42	8-Jan-43	20:55	VC
EE625	14-Oct-42	18-Jan-46	157:15	Clipped Wing 11/5/43
EE619	21-Jan-43	22-Jan-42	1:20	
EE611	18-Feb-43	19-Feb-43	2:15	
BE367	30-Apr-43	18-May-43	13:30	
CB	7-Sep-43	14-Nov-43	16:05	
NF482	20-Feb-44	12-Mar-44	2:25	IX
NE491	21-Feb-44	21-Feb-44	1:00	XIV

Description	1 seat fighter
Dimensions	Span 36ft 10in Length 29ft 11in
Performance	Max speed 357mph Range 400 miles
Armament	8 .303 guns

Supermarine Spitfire with a Griffon Engine

Number	Ist Flight	Last Flight	Hours	
MN333	17-Mar-44	19-Mar-44	3:00	XX
MK782	20-Mar-44	23-Feb-45	42:30	
SM756	13-Mar-45	13-Mar-45	0:30	XVI
XXI	31-Mar-45	31-Mar-45	0:30	
BL715	16-Apr-45	26-Apr-45	4:25	V
AB167	2-May-45	16-May-45	2:25	
TB301	26-Oct-46	5-Sep-47	12:45	XVI
SL721	9-Jun-49	2-Feb-51	85:50	XVI

Description	1 seat fighter
Dimensions	Span 40ft 2in Length 32ft 8in
Performance	Max speed 450mph Range 460 miles
Armament	8 .303 guns

22   Supermarine Seafire

26-Aug-47	26-Aug-47	0:40	XVII

Description	1 seat carrier borne fighter
Dimensions	Span 36ft 10in Length 32ft 8in
Performance	Max speed 450mph Range 460-850 m.
Armament	2 20mm 4 .303in guns 500lb bombs

23   North American Mustang

Number	1st Flight	Last Flight	Hours
AA513	30-Jun-42	30-Jun-42	0:30
259	9-Nov-42	9-Nov-42	0:30
925	15-Nov-42	15-Nov-42	1:30
AM129	31-Dec-42	31-Dec-42	1:30

Description	1 seat fighter fighter-bomber
Dimensions	Span 36ft 10in Length 32ft 8in
Performance	Max speed 450mph Range 950-1,700 miles.
Armament	2 20mm+ 2 .50 guns 1000lb bombs

24   de Havilland DH87 Hornet Moth

X1192	28-Jul-42	27-Aug-42	3:25

Description	2 seat side by side communications
Dimensions	Span 31ft 11in Length 24ft 11 1/2in
Performance	Max speed 124mph Range 620 miles

25   Hawker Typhoon

26-Aug-47	26-Aug-47	0:40	XVII

Description	1 seat fighter fighter bomber
Dimensions	Span 41ft 7in Length 31ft 11in
Performance	Max speed 412mph Range 510-980 miles.
Armament	4 20mm guns 2 1000lb bombs or 8 rockets

26   Miles Martinet

Number	Ist Flight	Last Flight	Hours
HP157	21-Dec-42	21-Dec-42	0:25

Description	2 seat target-tug
Dimensions	Span 39ft Length 30ft 11in
Performance	Max speed 240mph Range 694 miles

27   Airspeed Oxford

10-Jun-43	28-Jul-52	11:05

Description 3 seat advanced trainer communications
Dimensions Span 53ft 4in Length 34ft 6in
Performance Max speed 188mph

28   Percival Proctor

2-Jul-43	4-Aug-43	11:55
17-May-47	14-Sep-48	6:10

Description	4 seat radio trainer and communications
Dimensions	Span 39ft 6in Length 28ft 2in
Performance	Max speed 160mph Range 500 miles

29   General Aircraft Monospar

Number	Ist Flight	Last Flight	Hours
	11-Aug-43	10-Sep-43	2:30

Description	4 seat radio trainer and communications
Dimensions	Span 40ft 2in Length 26ft 4in
Performance	Max speed 130mph

30   Miles Monarch

16-Aug-43	6-Sep-43	5:20

Description 3 seat communications
Dimensions Span 35ft 7in Length 25ft 4in
Performance Max speed 140mph Range 600miles

31   Westland Whirlwind

16-Sep-43	16-Sep-43	0:30

Description	1 seat long-range fighter fighter-bomber
Dimensions	Span 45ft Length 32ft 9in
Performance	Max speed 360mph Range 800 miles
Armament	4 20mm guns 1000lb bomb load

32 de Havilland Dominie

Number	Ist Flight	Last Flight	Hours
K8104	24-Feb-44	28-Oct-46	6:20
	25-Jul-47	18-May-48	7:40
221	19-May-50	19-May-50	0:30

Description	5-10 seat radio navigation or communications
Dimensions	Span 48ft Length 34ft 6in
Performance	Max speed 157mph Range 570 miles

33 Gloster Meteor

Number	Ist Flight	Last Flight	Hours	Mark
	14-Jun-44	30-Jun-44	4:05	I
	14-Oct-49	23-Jun-52	11:15	IV
	14-Oct-49	15-May-52	3:40	VII
662	23-Feb-51	27-Feb-51	5:50	VII
656	12-Mar-51	15-May-52	19:15	VII
	23-Apr-58	31-Jul-58	2:35	

Description	1 seat interceptor fighter
Dimensions	Span 43ft Length 41ft 4in
Performance	Max speed 410mph
Armament	4 20mm guns

34   Douglas Dakota

Number	Ist Flight	Last Flight	Hours
	15-Jan-45	15-Jan-45	1:10
KK200	22-Feb-47	1-Jun-49	14:45

> **Description** 3 crew Military transport
> **Dimensions** Span 95ft Length 64ft 6in
> **Performance** Max speed 230mph Range 1,500 miles

35   Taylorcraft Auster

	15-Jan-45	15-Jan-45	1:10
KK200	22-Feb-47	1-Jun-49	14:45
33 NJ513	10-Apr-45	14-Apr-45	1:15
NJ615	14-Apr-45	14-Apr-45	0:40
RT533	15-Apr-45	16-Apr-45	1:45
RJ213	17-Apr-45	18-Apr-45	1:15
RJ409	19-Apr-45	19-Apr-45	0:50
RN617	8-May-45	8-May-45	2:00
TJ623	11-May-45	11-May-45	0:45
TJ417	14-May-45	23-Jul-45	2:40
TJ516	3-Sep-45	3-Sep-45	0:30
534	21-Jan-46	21-Jan-46	0:20
	8-Apr-52	4-Jun-52	5:00

> **Description** 3 seat Air Observation Post and communications
> **Dimensions** Span 36ft Length 22ft 5in
> **Performance** Max speed 130mph Range 250-300 miles

36   Hawker Tempest

Number	Ist Flight	Last Flight	Hours	
SN217	7-May-45	3-Nov-45	106:15	
AB187	24-May-45	2-Jun-45	4:00	
	16-Oct-45	16-Oct-45	0:30	II
103	19-Jan-46	19-Jan-46	1:4	

Description	1 seat fighter-bomber
Dimensions	Span 41ft Length 33ft 8in
Performance	Max speed 427mph Range 740-1,530 miles
Armament	4 20mm guns rocket-prjectiles or 2,000lb of bombs

37   Miles Messenger

10-Oct-45	10-Oct-45	0:50

Description 4 seat Liaison
Dimensions Span 36ft 2in Length 24ft
Performance Max speed 116mph Range 260miles

38   de Havilland Mosquito

560	21-Oct-45	26-Oct-45	3:00
TA524	1-Feb-46	7-Mar-46	3:40

Description	2 seat fighter-bomber
Dimensions	Span 54ft 2in Length 40ft 6in
Performance	Max speed 380mph Range 1300miles
Armament	4 20mm + 4 .303 guns 2 500lb bombs

39   Fieseler Storch

Number	Ist Flight	Last Flight	Hours
	22-Jan-46	13-Feb-46	3:15

Description	3 seat STOL observation and liaison
Dimensions	Span 46ft 9in Length 32ft 6in
Performance	Max speed 109mph Range 238miles

40   Avro York

	17-Feb-48	17-May-48	113:40

Description	5 crew 24 passenger long range transport
Dimensions	Span 102ft Length 78ft 6in
Performance	Max speed 298mph Range 2,700miles

41   de Havilland Vampire

Number	Ist Flight	Last Flight	Hours	
		1-Jul-49	11:20	
	16-Feb-51	16-Feb-51	1:20	K
	18-Feb-51	19-Feb-51	2:10	C
	20-Feb-51	20-Feb-51	0:55	F
	20-Feb-51	20-Feb-51	0:55	Y
150	24-Feb-51	5-Mar-51	2:10	
830	6-Mar-51	9-Nov-51	105:35	

Description	1 seat interceptor fighter
Dimensions	Span 40ft 6in Length 30ft 9in
Performance	Max speed 540mph Range 730miles
Armament	1 Forward 1 Aft .303 1 18in torpedo

.42   Vickers Viking

Number	Ist Flight	Last Flight	Hours
	31-Jan-50	1-Feb-50	2:30

Description	2/3 crew Passenger transport
Dimensions	Span 89ft 3in Length 65ft 2in
Performance	Max speed 210mph Range 1,700 miles

43   de Havilland DH-140 Dove

981	16-May-49	2-Feb-51	5:05

Description	2 crew light transport
Dimensions	Span 57ft Length 39ft 6in
Performance	Max speed 205mph

44   de Havilland Venom

14-Jun-51	14-Jun-51	0:40

Description	1 seat fighter-bomber
Dimensions	Span 41ft 8in Length 31ft 10in
Performance	Max speed 640mph Range 1,000miles
Armament	4 20 mm guns provision for 2,000lb bombs or rockets

Post RAF Flying
Joint British Australian Project
Defence Research Centre Salisbury
The Range Woomera

45   de Havilland Canada DHC3 Otter

Number	Ist Flight	Last Flight	Hours
	14-Feb-58	24-Jul-60	29:50

Description	1/2 crew utility transport
Dimensions	Span 58ft Length 41ft 10in
Performance	Max speed 160 mph Range 945 miles

46   Sud-Aviation Alouette

17-Feb-58	6-Oct-60	73:20

Description	crew 1+6 Mid-size helicopter
Dimensions	Rotor 36ft 2in Length 32ft 10in
Performance	Max speed 130 mph Range 300 miles

47   English Electric Canberra

Number	Ist Flight	Last Flight	Hours
	27-Apr-58	27-Apr-58	0:50

Description	2 seat light bomber intruder
Dimensions	Span 63ft 11in Length 65ft 6in
Performance	Max speed 541 mph Range 805 miles

48   Beechcraft Kingair

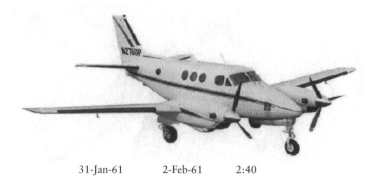

	31-Jan-61	2-Feb-61	2:40

Description	1/2 crew passenger
Dimensions	Span 45ft 10in Length 35ft 6in
Performance	Max speed 250 mph Range 1,550miles

BIBLIOGRAPHY

Primary Sources

Public Records Office

Air 2/8973	US Awards to RAF Personnel
Air 24/1497	2nd TAF
Air 25/182	10 Group HQ
Air 26	Ibsley Wing
Air 27	ORB 400 Squadron
Air 27/1598	276 Squadron
Air 27/1602	277 Squadron
Air 28	RAF Tangmere, Aug/Sept 1940
Air 28	RAF Tangmere, Sept 1942
Air 28	RAF Horsham St Faith, Mar 1944
Air 28/245	RAF Hawkinge
Air 28/395	RAF Ibsley, 1943/44
Air 28/954	RAF Woodbridge
Air 29/445	ASR Dover
Air 29/888	ASR Flight Hawkinge
Air 29/1833	Old Sarum School of Air/land Warfare
Air 29/1983	Air Ministry Unit, London
Air 29/2382	Air Ministry Unit, Kenley
Air 37/1	2nd TAF HQ
Air 42	Combined Operations Planning Committee
Air 50	Combat reports USAF
Air 50/19	ORB 43 Squadron
Air 50/411	Combat report T F Dalton Morgan
WO 373	Order of the British Empire

WO 390   Register of the DSO
HQ 4th Fighter Group AAF STA F-356
            Group History for March, April, May, June,
            July, August, September, October 1944

Tactical Mission Report, HQ 8th Air Force for 16 March 1944

RAF Pilots Log Book; G/Capt. T F Dalton Morgan

RAF Pilots Log Book; G/Capt. J W C Simpson

Selected Bibliography

Adam, Ronald, *Readiness at Dawn*, London 1941

Air Ministry, *The Battle of Britain*, HMSO 1941

Air Ministry, *The Rise and Fall of the German Air Force*, London 1946

Anthony, Gordon, and Macadam, John, *Air Aces*, London 1944

Austin, A B, *Fighter Command*, London 1941

Barrymaine, Norman, *The Story of Peter Townsend*, London 1958

Bartz, Karl, *Swastika in the Air*, London 1956

Baumbach, Werner, *Broken Swastika*, London 1960

Beckles, Gordon, *Birth of the Spitfire*, London 1941

Beedle J, *43 Squadron*, 1966

Bekker, Cajus, *The Luftwaffe Diaries*, London 1966

Bishop, Edward, *The Battle of Britain*, London 1960

Bolitho, Hector, *Combat Report*, London 1943

Boorman, H R Pratt, *Hell's Corner, 1940*, Maidstone 1942

Braybrooke, Keith, *Wingspan: A History of RAF Debden*, Saffron Walden 1956

Brickhill, Paul, *Reach for the Sky*, London 1954

Bungay, S, *The Most Dangerous Enemy*

Butler, Ewan, and Young, Gordon, *Marshal Without Glory*, London 1951

Carne, Daphne, *The Eyes of the Few*, London 1960

Chambers, E W, *Woomera as Human Face*, 2000

Charlton, L E O, *Britain at War: The Royal Air Force, September 1939 to September 1945*

Childers, James Saxon, *War Eagles*, New York 1943

Clout, Charles, *Swastika Over Sussex*, Air Britain Digest, March 1965

Cluett, D, Bogle, J, and Learmouth, B, *Croydon Airport and the*

Battle of Britain, Sutton 1984

Collier, Basil, *The Defence of the United Kingdom*, London 1957
    The Leader of the Few, London 1957
    The Battle of Britain, London 1962

Critzbach, Erich, *Hermann Göring: The Man and His Work*, London 1939

Crook, D M, *Spitfire Pilot*, London 1942

Deedman, J, *RAF Ibsley, 1941-47*, Parts 1 & 2, 1996/7

Deere, Alan, *Nine Lives*, London 1959

Dierich, Wolfgang, *Kampfgeschwader 51 'Edelweiss': Eine Chronik aus Dokumenten und Berichten, 1937-1945*, Stuttgart

Dempster, Derek, and Wood, Derek, *The Narrow Margin*, London 1961

Dowding, Air Chief Marshal the Lord, *The Battle of Britain*, (a supplement to the London Gazette 1946)

Embry, Sir basil, *Mission Completed*, London 1957

Farrer, David, *The Sky's the Limit, The Story of Beaverbrook at MAP*, London 1943

Fiedler, Arkady, *Squadron 303:The Story of the Polish Fighter Squadron with the RAF*, London 1942

Fleming, Peter, *Invasion 1940*, London 1957

Forbes, W/Cdr Athol, and Allen, S/Ldr Hubert, *Ten Fighter Boys*, London 1942

Forrester, Larry, *Fly For Your Life*, Bristol 2003

Foster, Reginald, *Dover Front*, London 1941

Freeman, R A, *The Mighty Eighth*, London 1970
    The Mighty Eighth Diary, London 1993
    The Mighty Eighth Manual

Friedin, Seymour (ed.) *The Fatal Decisions*, New York 1956

Fry, C C, and Ethel, J L, *Escort to Berlin*, London 1980

Galland, Adolf, *The First and the Last*, Bristol 2003

Gallico, Paul, *The Hurricane Story*, London 1959

Garnett, David, *War in the Air*, London 1941

Gleed, Ian, *Arise to Conquer*, London 1942

Graves, Charles, *The Home Guard of Britain*, London 1943
    The Thin Blue Line, London 1941

Griffith, Hubert, *RAF Occasions*, London 1941

Hall,Grover C, *1,000 Destroyed*, London 1962

Hillary, Richard, *The Last Enemy*, London 1942

James, T C G, *The Battle of Britain*, London 2000

Johnson, Air Vice-Marshal, J E, *Full Circle*, London 1964

Joubert, Air Chief Marshal Sir Philip, *The Forgotten Ones*, London 1961

Kempe, A B C, *Midst Bands and Bombs*, Maidstone 1946

Kennedy, A Scott, *'Gin Ye Daur': 603 squadron (City of Glasgow) Fighter Squadron*, Edinburgh 1943

Kesselring, Generalfeldmarschall Albert, *Memoirs*, London 1953

Knöke, Heinz, *I Flew for the Führer*, London 1952

Lee, Asher, *The German Air Force*, London 1946

Lewey, F R, *Cockney Campaign*, London 1953

Lloyd, F H M, *Hurricane: The Story of a Great Fighter*, London 1953

McCrary, John R (Tex), and Scherman, David E, *First of the Many*, New York 1944

Mackenzie, W/Cdr K W, *Hurricane Combat*, London 1987

Macmillan, W/Cdr Norman, *The Royal Air Force in the World War*, Vol. I-II, London 1942-44

Manvell, Roger, and Fraenkel, Heinrich, *Hermann Göring*, London 1962

Mason, Francis K, *Battle over Britain*, London 1969

Masters, David, *'So Few'* (8th edition), London 1946

Middleton, Drew, *The Sky Suspended*, London 1960

Miller, Kent D, *Fighter Units & Pilots of the 8th Air Force*, Vol. 1 & 2, New York 2001

Moulson, T, *The Flying Sword: The Story of No. 601 Squadron*, London 1964

Newton, John H, *The Story of No. 11 Group*, ROC, Lincoln 1946

Obermeier, Ernst, *Die Ritterkreuzträger der Luftwaffe: Jagdflieger, 1939-45*, Mainz 1966
Die Ritterkreuzträger der Luftwaffe: Stuka-und Schlactflieger, 1939-45, Mainz 1976

O'Brien, T H, *Civil Defence*, London 1955

Orange, Vincent, *Sir Keith Park*, London 1984
Coningham, London 1990

Orde, Cuthbert, *Pilots of Fighter Command*, London 1942

Parker, M, *The Battle of Britain, July-Oct 1940*, London 2001

Pile, General Sir Frederick, *Ack-Ack*, London 1949

Price, Alfred, *Instruments of Darkness*, London 1967

Priller, Josef, *Geschichte eines Jagdgeschwaders (Das JG26, 1937-45)*, Heidelberg 1962

Ramsey, W G (ed.) *The Battle of Britain Then and Now*, After the Battle 1989

Rawlings, John, *Fighter Squadrons of the RAF and their Aircraft*, London 1969

Rawnsley, C F, and Wright, Robert, *Night Fighter*, London 1957

Reed, S, *G/Capt. T F Dalton-Morgan, DSO, OBE, DFC* Unpublished manuscript

Reid, J P M, *Some of the Few*, London 1960

Richards, Denis, *Royal Air Force, 1939-45*. Vol. I, *The Fight at Odds*, London 1953

Ring, Hans, and Girbig, Werner, *Jagdgeschwader 27: Die Dokumentation über den Einsatz an allen Fronten,1939-1945*, Stuttgart 1971

Shores, Christopher, & Williams, Clive, *Aces High: The Fighter Aces of British & Commonwealth Air Forces in World War II*, Spearman 1966, reprinted and updated, Grub Street, 1994

Saunders, A, *No. 43 'Fighting Cocks' Squadron*, 2002

Saunders, Hilary St George, *The Battle of Britain*, London 1942

Slessor, Marshal of the RAF Sir John, *The Central Blue*, London 1956

Spaight, J M, *The Battle of Britain*, London 1941
             The Sky is the Limit, London 1940

Speer, Hank E, *The Debden Warbirds*. New York 1999

Townsend, Peter, *Duel of Eagles*, London 1960

Wolf, William, *USAAF Jabos in the MTO and ETO*, New York 2003

Wykeham, Air Vice-Marshal Peter, *Fighter Command*, London 1960

INDEX